SINGER®
DESIGN SERIES

f·a·b·r·i·c
ARTISTRY

COWLES
Creative Publishing

Copyright © 1998 Cowles Creative Publishing, Inc.
5900 Green Oak Drive, Minnetonka, Minnesota 55343 • 1-800-328-3895 • All rights reserved • Printed in U.S.A.

SINGER®
DESIGN
SERIES

fa·b·r·i·c

ARTISTRY!

Table of Contents

FABRIC ARTISTRY

Created by: The Editors
of Cowles Creative Publishing, Inc., in cooperation with the Sewing
Education Department, Singer Sewing Company. Singer is a trademark
of The Singer Company Limited and is used under license.

Library of Congress Cataloging-in-Publication Data
Fabric artistry.
        p. cm. -- (Singer design series)
    Includes index.
    ISBN 0-86573-323-6 (hardcover). -- ISBN 0-86573-326-0 (softcover)
    1. Textile crafts. 2. Fancy work. 3. Clothing and dress.
4. House furnishings. I. Cowles Creative Publishing. II. Series.
TT699.F32 1998
746--dc21   97-48864

INTRODUCTION

Most of us were taught to approach a sewing project by finding an appealing pattern and then searching for fabric in a suitable color, print design, fiber content, and weave structure. Or we purchase a "must have" fabric and the next step is to find or design a suitable pattern. In contrast, the artist's approach to designing a garment or soft furnishing for the home begins with the fabric itself. Fabric is selected on its merits as an open canvas for the artist's creativity, waiting for an inspired hand to alter its character and define its purpose. Surface texture, print design, and hand are traits that the artist can change and develop in the creative process. A pattern is selected or developed in a simple style that best exhibits the artist's work and allows for individual expression.

There is a creative artist dwelling inside each and every one of us, longing for the opportunity to thrive and grow. As an important first step to freeing your creativity, learn to think of yourself as talented and capable, because you truly are. We invite you to admire and muse over the many splendid garments and home decorating elements throughout the Artists' Gallery of Inspirations, each expressing unique personality and style. The fabrics, techniques, and embellishments used for each project are the personal choices made by the artist. Take inspiration from these artists, knowing that their creations are the results of personal journeys of artistic discovery.

As you embark on your own journey of artistic discovery, use the instructions and photographs in the Techniques section as a springboard to exploration. Allow yourself the luxury of experimenting with various techniques, understanding that you may take an instant dislike to some and be immediately enthralled by others. Turn undesirable results into positive experiences; consider mistakes to be valuable learning tools to help you make choices. Develop a unique creative style all your own and express yourself through personal artistry. Just be forewarned; creative play can lead to addiction. There are no limits to your enjoyment, and once the creative artist in you is released, you may find time for little else!

Acknowledgment

We at Cowles Creative Publishing wish to express our sincere gratitude to the fabric artists who so generously allowed us to photograph their creations. Thank you for sharing your ideas, your dreams, and your talents as inspiration for our readers.

ARTISTS'
GALLERY
of
inspirations

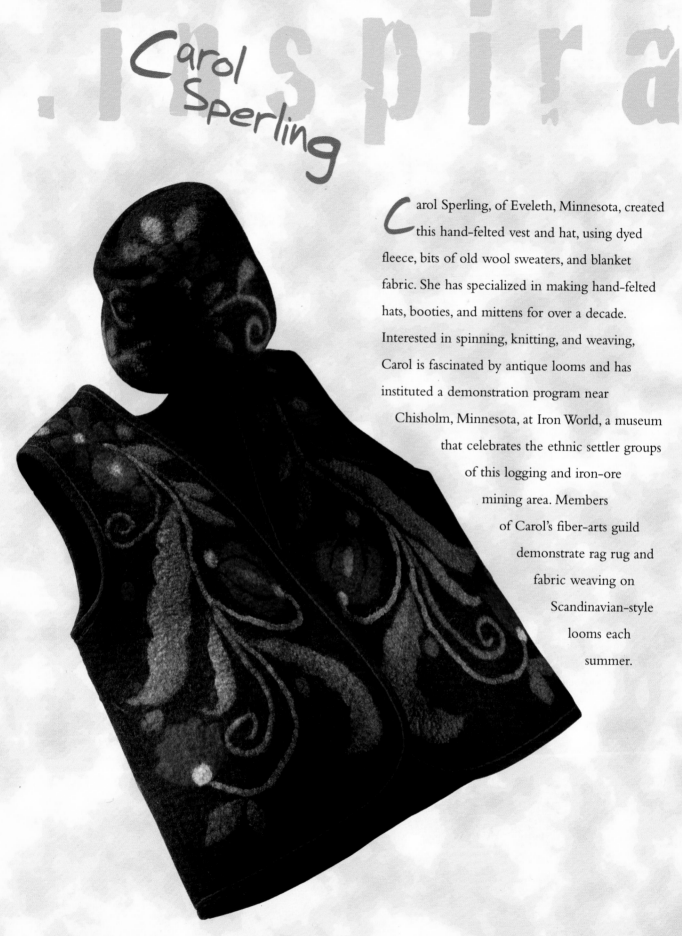

Carol Sperling

*C*arol Sperling, of Eveleth, Minnesota, created this hand-felted vest and hat, using dyed fleece, bits of old wool sweaters, and blanket fabric. She has specialized in making hand-felted hats, booties, and mittens for over a decade. Interested in spinning, knitting, and weaving, Carol is fascinated by antique looms and has instituted a demonstration program near Chisholm, Minnesota, at Iron World, a museum that celebrates the ethnic settler groups of this logging and iron-ore mining area. Members of Carol's fiber-arts guild demonstrate rag rug and fabric weaving on Scandinavian-style looms each summer.

Katherine Tilton

Katherine Tilton, owner of Tilton's Tease in St. Paul, Minnesota, is the designer of this felted wool coat and the jacket on the back cover. Both feature raw-edge appliqué and hand-painted binding. Katherine designs eclectic hand-painted clothing and objects, which have appeared in many exhibitions and collections. She has taught art and art-to-wear classes for children in Minnesota public schools and through the St. Paul Museum of American Art. She has also created and taught art classes and workshops for adults, served as a consultant on several Singer® Sewing Reference Library® books, and worked with the COMPAS/Minnesota Coalition for Battered Women Open Book Project, where she developed the model for an art project and statewide exhibition for children in shelters.

...inspira

in
Lin Lacy

Lin Lacy, a Twin Cities, Minnesota, fiber artist, "paints" in multimedia, creating wall hangings, art clothing and decorative objects. She has worked in interior design, created costumes for the Minnesota Opera Company, and restored museum tapestries. Lin is known for her use of recycled clothing, jewelry, and household items to create unique wearable art, adorned with appliqué, beading, and embroidery. This winter ensemble exhibits Lin's creative knack with felted wool, couched yarns, and beading.

Gini
Corrick

Gini Corrick of Crosslake, Minnesota, designed this silk blouse, which features texturized fabric with decorative stitching and beadwork. Gini describes herself as a "sewist," having had a love affair with fabric since childhood. In addition to participating in and twice serving as director of the Airstream International Rally Fashion Show, Gini has organized sewing seminars for that group and has conducted annual wearable art shows for the Pinetree Patchworkers of Brainerd, Minnesota.

Jane Conlon

Jane Conlon sews, writes, and teaches in Eugene, Oregon. Enchanted with the practical and creative challenges that sewing provides, she consistently strives for artfulness that is apparent in the attention to detail and workmanship of the garment. Her techniques include fabric weaving, machine-stitched and hand-stitched embroidery, appliqués, and beadwork embellishments. This pin-woven vest is a prime example of her ability to work decorative details into the garment design. Some of Jane's work, including the Celtic appliqué and trapunto designs below, has appeared in *Threads* magazine.

P in weaving and double-needle stitching are combined in this elegant table runner, designed and sewn by members of the Cowles Creative Publishing home arts staff. Fabric artistry techniques give home fashions designer appeal while giving your decorating scheme a personal touch.

Julann Windsperger

Julann Windsperger, who has been sewing since before she started school, has combined a 25-year nursing career with a home-based business, Julann's Stitchery. Since 1990, she has been creating unique quilted and pieced garments, like the one at left. Julann works nights in a Minnesota hospital transplant unit and days designing and stitching on her industrial quilting machine — as she says, "What excitement!"

Linda Nelson Bryan

Linda Nelson Bryan is an award–winning textile artist. She has maintained a studio in St. Paul since receiving her Masters in Textile Design from the University of Minnesota in 1974. Her works encompass an amalgam of varied surface design techniques and aesthetic approaches. In this dress, Linda has combined various dyeing techniques with a rhythmic flowing cascade of double–needle pintucks. Linda has exhibited internationally and has participated in a number of artist residencies, including several years with COMPAS, in St. Paul, and a summer spent at the Fiberarts Interchange at the Banff Centre for the Arts, Canada. For ten years, she taught Surface Design at the University of Minnesota and currently is an instructor, teaching Fiber Structure courses.

Penelope Trudeau

Penelope D. Trudeau, of New
Hope, Minnesota, took an early
retirement, after a long career in
hospital management and a degree in
law, to devote her time to quilting —
creating wall quilts and garments in
order to express herself through fiber
and "bring art and beauty. . .peace and
calm. . .into other people's lives."
Her art, represented by the coat
at left, combines original design,
fabric painting and dyeing,
and many needlework skills.
She agrees with a friend,
who said, "There is no
finer place to show
art than on your
back!"

Justine Limpus Parish

Justine Limpus Parish, of South Pasadena, California, has worked in the fashion industry as an illustrator, art director, designer, and educator. She created the Fashion Department at the Academy of Art College in San Francisco, lectures and teaches workshops on Innovative Design, and is the author of *Drawing the Fashion Body*. She currently produces a line of Shibori hand-pleated and color-accented garments, such as this coat and dress ensemble, featured in specialty stores nationwide.

Joan Wigginton

Joan Kees Wigginton, a professional interior designer from Plymouth, Minnesota, started sewing on her grandmother's Singer® treadle machine, beginning with doll's clothes and later designing gowns for friends' high school dances. She has taught adult education sewing-construction classes and continues to design clothes and explore new materials and design details. Her jacket was inspired by her love of diving into the undersea world and by the book, *Quilted Sea Tapestries*, by Ginny Eckley.

Marian Hehre

Marian Hehre, of Minneapolis, Minnesota, began sewing at an early age, influenced by her grandmother. An avid quilter since 1982, Marian has gradually moved from traditional styles to wearable art, as demonstrated by her unique jackets, above and on page 2. She teaches a variety of classes to all ages and has won several awards for her designs. A common thread through all of Marian's activities is her ability to move herself and others beyond traditional boundaries, view mistakes as creative opportunities, and truly enjoy the creative process.

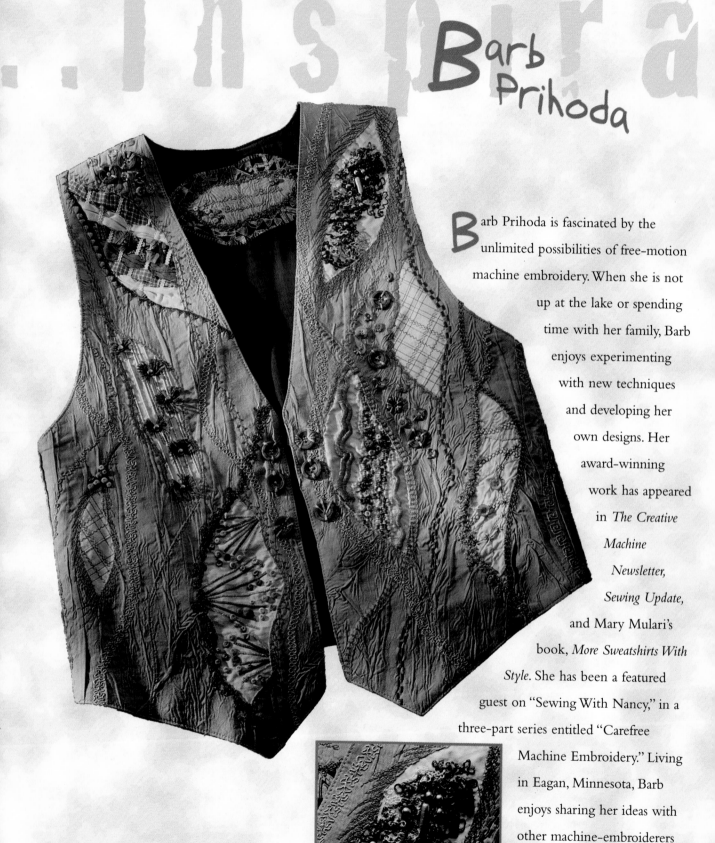

...inspira

Barb Prihoda

Barb Prihoda is fascinated by the unlimited possibilities of free-motion machine embroidery. When she is not up at the lake or spending time with her family, Barb enjoys experimenting with new techniques and developing her own designs. Her award-winning work has appeared in *The Creative Machine Newsletter, Sewing Update,* and Mary Mulari's book, *More Sweatshirts With Style.* She has been a featured guest on "Sewing With Nancy," in a three-part series entitled "Carefree Machine Embroidery." Living in Eagan, Minnesota, Barb enjoys sharing her ideas with other machine-embroiderers around the country.

Coralie Sathre

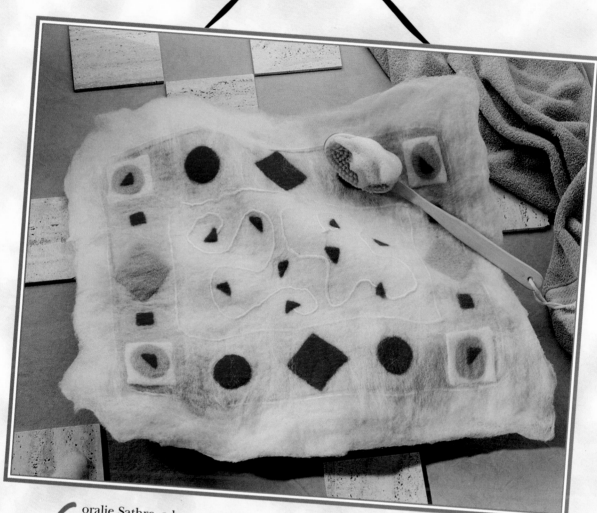

oralie Sathre, a home arts staff member of Cowles Creative Publishing, designed and felted this wool bath rug. Making felted wool is a new venture for her, one that seems to be a natural fit, considering her degree in Fine Arts and her love for the tactile and visual pleasures of fiber arts. Among her many interests, Coralie enjoys hand knitting and loom weaving.

𝐄mbossed rayon velvet edged with opulent bullion fringe gives this window swag a look of total elegance. The swag was designed, embossed, and sewn by members of the Cowles Creative Publishing home arts staff.

Iris Lee

Iris Lee, of Macon, Georgia, who began sewing on a treadle machine, taught fine arts, crafts, and needlework for 20 years before realizing the "infinite possibilities" of the new computerized machines, new threads, and new techniques of machine embroidery; she envisions a creative linkup between the personal computer and the sewing machine. She has taught her cutwork and decorative techniques since 1990 and has described them in two books; *Threads* magazine; and a video, "Artwork & Needlelace."

Random-cut fabric weaving and quilted effects were among the techniques used by members of the Cowles Creative Publishing home arts staff to design and sew this luxurious wool pillow. Their concerted efforts produced a celebration of textures, colors, and fabric artistry.

Margaret Andolshek

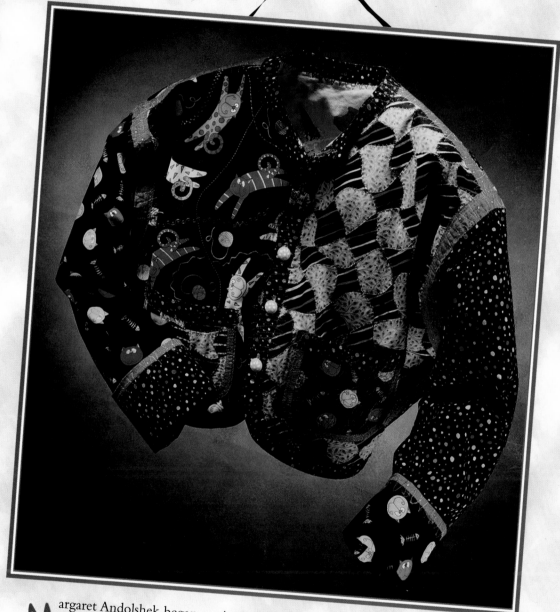

Margaret Andolshek began sewing when she was nine years old. After moving from the East Coast to Minnetonka, Minnesota, Margaret joined several sewing clubs and began taking sewing and fabric-manipulation classes. She continually challenges herself to try new techniques and shares her knowledge by teaching adult classes at the fabric store where she works.

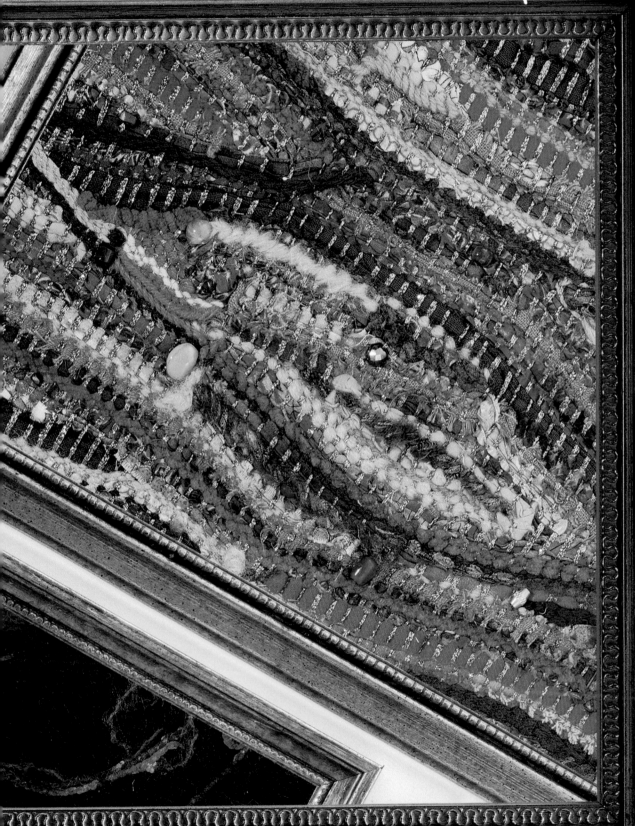

MAKING FELT

Felt is a nonwoven fabric made from wool fibers. You can design and make your own felt fabric, using precarded and predyed wool, called *roving* or *wool tops*. Carding means that the fibers have been combed so that all are running in the same direction. You will find roving in a variety of colors, from brights to subtle earth tones. It is available in many yarn stores, especially those that sell weaving and spinning supplies. Or it can be purchased through mail-order sources (page 112).

Making felt is a three-stage process, beginning with laying out the fibers in soft, lofty layers. The fibers in each layer must run perpendicular to the layer beneath them, in order for them to interlock and felt together. This is also the stage in which the design of the fabric is determined. The fibers are exposed to water, heat, and pressure in the *felting* stage, causing them to mat together to form a loose fabric. Further agitation and pressure, applied during the *fulling* stage, causes the fabric to shrink and harden into dense, strong felt. The actual process of making felt

takes a little "elbow grease," patience, and some readily available supplies. It is fascinating to watch and feel the fibers transforming under your fingers.

The amount of roving required for a project depends not only on the finished size, but also on the desired density. Roughly estimated, 1 ounce (25 g) of roving will produce a 12" × 12" (30.5 × 30.5 cm) square of felt. The best way to determine the amount of roving needed for a project is to make a small test sample first. Take note of the weight of roving used in the sample, the size of the sample before felting, and the amount of shrinkage. Use these findings to estimate the amount of roving needed for a larger project.

MATERIALS

- Wool roving.
- Reed mat; placemat, for small projects, window blind or beach mat for larger projects.
- Soap, such as Ivory Snow® or Murphy's Oil Soap®; mix ¼ cup (50 ml) soap with 1 quart (1 L) hot water.

- Pitcher, for mixing and pouring soap mixture.
- Plastic drop cloth.
- Synthetic screen netting.
- Wooden dowel, ¾" to 1" (2 to 2.5 cm) thick.

- Cotton sheeting.
- Kitchen scale, for measuring ounces of roving.
- Towels.

how_to Lay out Roving

2 Pull off small amount from first clump. Tease out fibers into even layer, thin enough to see through; place on mat. Repeat with small amounts, laying out teased pieces of uniform thickness next to each other. Run all fibers in same direction.

1 Cover work surface with plastic drop cloth. Place reed mat on drop cloth. Weigh ½ ounce (15 g) roving; divide into three clumps.

4 Lay out third layer, pulling small amounts from last clump. Run all fibers perpendicular to second layer, teasing pieces to uniform thickness.

3 Lay out second layer, pulling small amounts from second clump. Run all fibers perpendicular to first layer, teasing pieces to uniform thickness.

32

2 Moisten hands with soap mixture. Begin rubbing near center of netting, lightly at first, then applying increasing pressure. Work outward, rubbing entire area.

1 Cover roving layers entirely with synthetic screen netting. Sprinkle about 1 cup (250 mL) hot water (as hot as you can stand) over netting. Sprinkle 2 tablespoons (25 mL) soap mixture over netting, near center.

3 Continue rubbing two minutes; gently lift netting from fleece, making sure fibers do not stick to screen. Replace netting; continue rubbing. Add more hot water as needed to keep piece warm. Wipe away excess cool water; piece should be wet but not floating in water. Add soap mixture as needed to keep piece slippery.

4 Continue rubbing. After five minutes, lift netting and begin checking felting progress; pinch a few fibers and lift. If fibers come away from layers, continue felting. If entire piece lifts off mat, move on to fulling stage.

2 Roll the felt and mat together around the wooden dowel.

1 Wipe towel across netting to remove excess soap and water. Remove netting from felt.

3 Roll cotton sheeting around rolled mat. Begin rolling mat back and forth on work surface, applying as much pressure as you can. Felt will shrink in direction it is rolled.

4 Continue rolling and applying pressure. After two minutes, unroll mat; turn felt 90°. Reroll mat and felt together around dowel; roll mat in cotton sheeting. Continue rolling and applying pressure.

5 Repeat step 4 until felt has become hard and will not change shape easily when pulled. Remove fulled felt from mat; rinse out soap under cold running water. Roll up in towel to squeeze out excess moisture.

6 Lay felt on ironing board; cover with press cloth. Press with hot dry iron. This will make the felt smooth and flat with hard surface. Allow to dry thoroughly.

how to Make Designs in Felt

Lay out three layers of fibers for background, as in steps 1 to 4 on page 32. Add thin tufts of another color roving for delicate gradation of color. Twist fleece into loose rope to create line of color. Cut shapes from felt colors previously made; lay shapes in design. Add accents, such as wool yarn, silk or rayon threads, or snippets of fabric, covering nonwool items with light layer of wool fibers to adhere them to felt. Felt and full as on pages 33 and 34.

before

after

FELTED WOOL

Felted wools, both woven and knitted, can be used for creative piecing or embellishment. Any wool fabric that has not been treated to resist shrinkage can be felted. Pure wool works best, though you may successfully felt some blends that contain no more than 20% synthetic fibers. Old wool sweaters, especially multicolored and patterned styles, often produce very interesting felted results. Check out the sale tables for wool fabrics; often fabric that is rejected for its color or pattern will take on a more appealing character once it is felted. Experiment with various weave patterns and yarn types, such as bouclés, mohairs, tweeds, and heathers, to produce felted fabrics with various textures and appearances.

Hot water, agitation, and detergent work together to felt the wool. Several garments or pieces of fabric with similar colors can be felted at the same time. Cut away any linings, waistbands, or facings and take down hems, to allow the garment fabric to felt evenly. To prevent sweater sleeves from being stretched, turn them to the inside of the garment or place the sweater in a pillow-case and tie it closed. Placing garments in pillowcases also traps excess lint. Wash the wool in a full cycle in hot water, using the same amount of detergent you would use for laundering. Repeat the washing until the wool has felted to the desired appearance. It is difficult to distinguish the right from the wrong side of fully felted wool, and grainlines will disappear. However, you may still detect some knit patterns, such as cables and ribbing. Remove the garments from the pillowcases, shake out any excess lint, and tumble dry at a high temperature. The felting process produces a lot of lint, so be sure to clean the lint traps on your washing machine and dryer frequently and tie a nylon stocking over the end of the drain hose.

Press the felted wool from both sides, using a steam iron and a press cloth, and allow the fabric to dry thoroughly before using it. Once felted, the fabric will not ravel, though you may apply a decorative serged edge finish, if desired. Felted wool lends itself naturally to techniques such as raw-edge appliqué (page 39) or butted piecing (opposite). Use a size 90/14 or a 100/16 needle for sewing felted wool.

how_to Sew Pieced Felted Wool Appliqués

1 Cut felted wool pieces for each section of appliqué. Thread machine with wash-away thread, using regular thread in bobbin. Butt two adjoining pieces; stitch together, using wide zigzag stitch. Repeat for each butted seam.

2 Thread machine with rayon embroidery thread. Stitch over butted seams, using decorative machine stitch.

(continued)

3 Spray appliqué with water to remove wash-away thread. Steam lightly; allow to dry.

4 Position appliqué on background fabric; pin. Blindstitch around outer edge of appliqué, using invisible thread. (Contrasting thread was used to show detail.)

5 Couch (page 80) decorative cording or yarn over invisible stitching around outer edge of appliqué. Stitch in continuous lines, if possible.

6 Layer appliqués, if desired, for dimensional effect.

2 Stitch over stitching line from wrong side of garment, using decorative thread in the bobbin (page 84), or couch (page 80) decorative cording or yarn over stitching line on right side.

1 Cut appliqué shapes; position on background fabric as desired. Secure with glue stick. Stitch ⅛" to ¼" (3 to 6 mm) from edge, using invisible thread.

Seams in Felted Wool ～～～～～～～～～～～～～～～～～～～～～～

Lapped seams. Trim seam allowance from one edge; lap over adjoining edge up to seamline. Pin, or secure with basting tape. Topstitch close to edge. Stitch again ¼" (6 mm) from first row of stitching. Trim excess seam allowance on inside of garment.

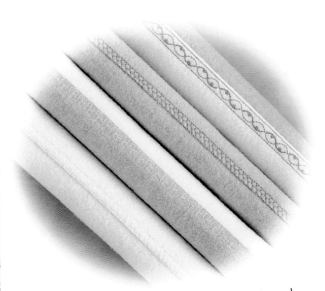

Decorative seams. Follow directions as for lapped seams, stitching seam with one row of decorative machine stitches instead of two straight-stitch rows.

PIN WEAVING

Pin weaving is a portable weaving method that resembles loom weaving in many ways. In fact, almost any effect you can create with loom weaving can be duplicated in pin weaving. The terms are similar, the techniques are easily adapted, and you don't have to be an experienced weaver or spend a lot of money on equipment to get great results. With pin weaving, fabric can be woven to the exact size and shape of the desired piece, following a pattern outline on the "loom" surface. This allows you to weave accent pieces for garment sections, such as pocket flaps, yokes, lapels, cuffs, and collars. Pillows, table runners, and wall hangings are also suitable projects and provide opportunities for design creativity.

The "loom" in pin weaving consists of pins inserted into a padded, gridded board, to hold the warp yarns. These boards, also used for tasks like pressing quilt blocks and blocking needlework, are available at sewing supply stores, quilt shops, and through mail-order catalogs. If you want to try pin weaving before investing in a padded board, an inexpensive, but effective, version can be made by adhering grid paper to foam-core board.

Depending on the intended location for the pin-woven section and the method by which it will be sewn into the project, you may want to fuse it to lightweight knit interfacing. This is most easily done by applying the interfacing, fusible side up, to the loom surface before pinning the warp. After the piece is woven, it can be

Warp is the arrangement of strong, usually parallel yarns that establishes the form and provides the strength for the woven piece. In woven fabric, the warp is the lengthwise direction, parallel to the selvages. When using a commercial pattern, you may warp the yarns parallel to the marked lengthwise grainline or perpendicular to it on the crosswise grainline. Or, for creative design purposes, you may wish to establish a new grain direction.

Place warp pins on the seamline to weave fabric to an exact shape with a finished edge. To weave fabric to an exact shape with finished seam allowances, place warp pins on the cutting line, as determined on page 43, step 4. Or place pins 1" to 2" (2.5 to 5 cm) beyond the seamlines to weave oversized fabric that will be cut to shape.

Weft consists of all the elements that are interlaced with the warp, passing over and under it in a systematic way to produce the desired woven design. Weft materials can include decorative yarns, cords and threads, narrow strips of fabric or leather, ribbons, or any other similar material. The weft can be manipulated in any direction except parallel to the warp and can change direction anywhere in the piece.

Weave with continuous weft material, looping over the last warp yarn at each side and returning in the opposite direction, to create selvages. Or weave with the weft material cut 1" to 2" (2.5 to 5 cm) longer than the pattern width to create oversized fabric that will be cut to shape.

Shed is the space formed in the warp to allow easy insertion of the weft material. A narrow stick is woven across the warp in the pattern intended for the weft material. When the stick is turned on edge, it opens the warp, allowing the shuttle, bodkin, or needle room to pass through, carrying the weft material.

Beating is the action of packing or compressing the weft materials to the desired tightness, using a wide-toothed comb, fork, or the fingers. The weft tightness may vary throughout the piece, if desired, creating added design interest. When you pin-weave with ribbons or flat fabric strips, if the desired look is to keep the ribbons or strips flat in their full width, the piece is not beaten.

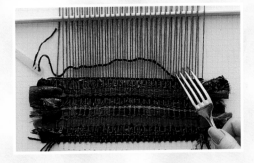

fused to the interfacing before removing it from the loom, thus ensuring that its shape will not be altered. This is especially suitable for large pieces loosely woven with weft materials, like ribbons and flat fabric strips. Fusible interfacing is also used anytime you intend to weave an oversized piece and then cut it to a desired shape. However, interfacing is not necessary for smaller pieces that are woven to shape, especially if the weft is fairly tightly compressed or if the piece will be lined.

Pieces can be woven with or without seam allowances, depending on how they will be used. Buttonholes or pocket slits can be created as you weave. Also, since the final shape and all design lines are outlined on the loom surface just under the warp, you can begin weaving in any area desired, perhaps creating strong design interest first, and then filling in unwoven areas later.

- **Padded, gridded pinning board** or ¼" or ½" (6 mm or 1.3 cm) foam-core board and ¼" or ½" (6 mm or 1.3 cm) grid paper and adhesive.

- **Sturdy straight pins** with small heads.

- **Pin-weaving shuttle** or bodkin, large-eyed blunt needle, or elastic guide.

- **Narrow, flat wooden stick,** for creating a shed.

- **Warp thread,** such as pearl cotton, carpet warp, or cotton yarn.

- **Weft materials,** such as fabric strips, ribbons, yarns, cords, or threads.

- **Beads,** optional.

- **Fine-gauge wire,** for attaching beads to warp cord.

- **Beating tool,** such as wide-toothed comb or fork.

how to Pin-weave

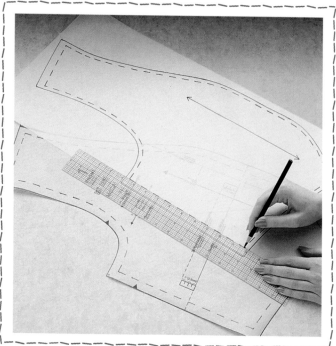

1 Trace pattern seamline onto tracing paper. Trace any darts along stitching lines. Mark any buttonholes or other slits. Mark desired grainline. Draw cutting line ¼" (6 mm) beyond seamline for finished curved edges that will be sewn into a seam or finished edges that will be sewn to lining; draw standard cutting lines on edges that will be cut to size and sewn into garment. Omit step 2 if using purchased pinning board.

2 Adhere grid paper to foam-core board or draw grid directly on board.

3 Pin prepared pattern faceup on board, aligning desired grainline to grid. If woven piece will be interfaced, preshrink interfacing. Cut interfacing larger than pattern; place fusible side up over pattern.

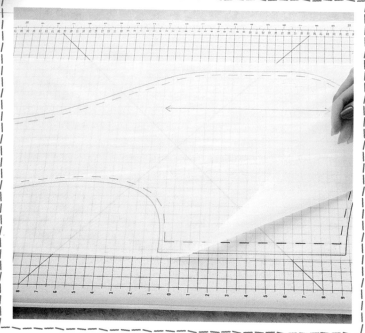

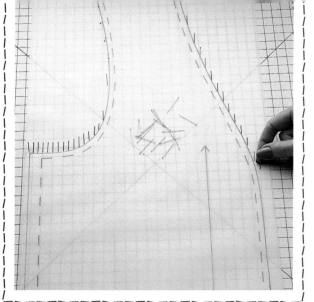

4 Insert warp pins through interfacing and pattern, into board at sharp angle away from pattern. Insert pins along stitching line to create finished edge or along cutting lines, following grid; leave pin heads extending ½" (1.3 cm) from surface. Space pins ¼" to ½" (6 mm to 1.3 cm) apart, depending on the bulkiness of warp yarns and weft materials.

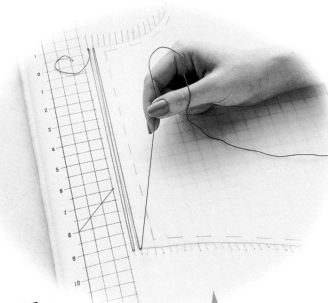

5 Attach warp yarn to corner pin, using slipknot. Keeping even, taut tension, wrap warp yarn back and forth from top to bottom, wrapping around each pin in turn. Secure to last pin with slipknot.

6 Check warp for even tension by running fingers across warp. Tighten any loose warp yarns by moving pin slightly outward.

7 Create shed (page 41), weaving it in plain weave pattern (page 45) near center of loom. Turn shed on edge, separating warp yarns.

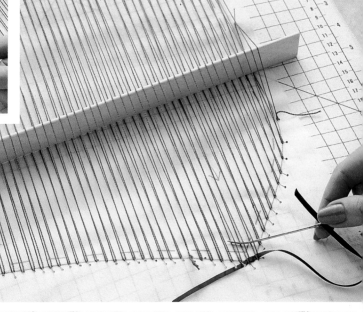

(continued)

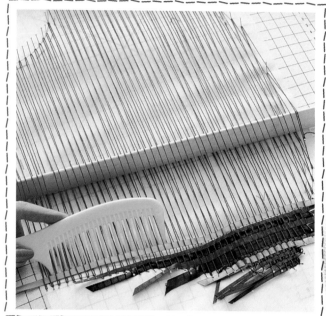

8 Insert weft materials through shed, using shuttle, if desired, and inserting weft in an arc. Beat weft into position against lower warp pins.

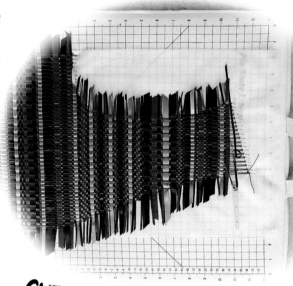

9 Weave piece in desired weave patterns (opposite), creating desired design details (pages 46 and 47). Beat weft materials to desired tightness. Complete piece with at least one row of plain weave next to top warp pins. Omit step 10 if piece will not be interfaced.

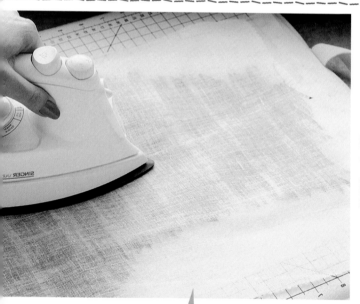

11 Remove pins. If piece is interfaced, place facedown on pressing surface; press again to completely fuse interfacing. Sew piece into project as desired.

10 Cover woven piece with press cloth; press lightly to partially fuse interfacing to piece.

Basic Weave Patterns ∿∿∿∿∿∿∿∿∿∿∿

Basket Weave. Pass weft over two warp yarns, under next two, over next two, continuing in this pattern across row. Repeat the pattern with the second row; reverse the pattern with the following two rows. Continue weaving, changing pattern every two rows.

Plain Weave. Pass weft over one warp, under next, over next, continuing in this pattern across row. Reverse the pattern with each succeeding row.

Twill Weave. Pass the weft over two warp yarns, under one, over two, under one, continuing across row. In the second weft row, and each succeeding row, shift the pattern one warp yarn to the right, creating a diagonal pattern.

Rib Weave. Pass weft over two warp yarns, under two, over two, under two, continuing in this pattern across row. Reverse the pattern with each succeeding row.

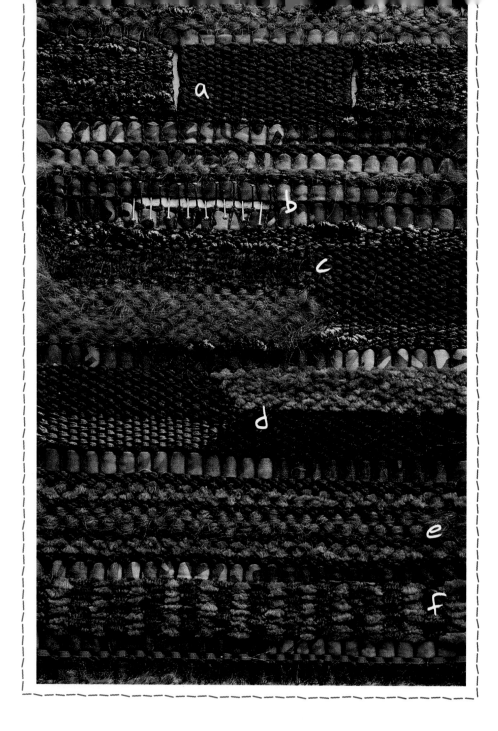

Weaving Design Details

Vertical Slits (a). Plain weave up to the desired slit opening, weaving with separate weft yarns from right and left. Circle the adjacent warp yarns, and weave weft yarns back to their origins, continuing the plain weave. Continue weaving and meeting at same warp yarns until desired slit length is completed. Weave above and below slits with weft yarns that cross entire row.

Horizontal Slits (b). When setting up the warp, insert two additional rows of pins, angled in opposite directions, along marked slit line. String the warp from the top of the project to the top of the slit, and from the bottom of the project to the bottom of the slit. Weave first weft rows above and below slit in plain weave pattern.

Hatching (c) is used to gradually merge one color or type of weft material into another. Start each color on same row on opposite sides of warp. Vary meeting points for several rows, like interlocking fingers, keeping the meetings random, to avoid forming slits. Leave short tails of weft material on back of woven piece.

Dovetailing (d) is similar to hatching, but the meeting warps are planned to create a repeating design.

Stripes. Create horizontal stripes **(e)** by plain weaving several weft rows of solid color, alternated with several contrasting rows. Create vertical stripes **(f)** by alternating weft colors every row in plain weave.

Combining Ribbons and Yarns (g). Create shed in desired weave pattern. Insert ribbons strips to loosely fill lower half of warp, stacking strips one above the other. Remove shed. Weave weft yarns or decorative cords between ribbon strips, in opposite weave pattern from ribbon strips. For added interest, weave weft, using chaining, Soumak, Egyptian knots, or Oriental Soumak (pages 48 and 49).

Free-flowing Designs (h). Insert desired weft materials in various weave patterns and shapes to create strong design lines throughout piece. Weave smaller-scale, varied weft materials around strong design lines, filling in empty spaces. Beat weft materials to desired tightness, varying tightness throughout piece, if desired.

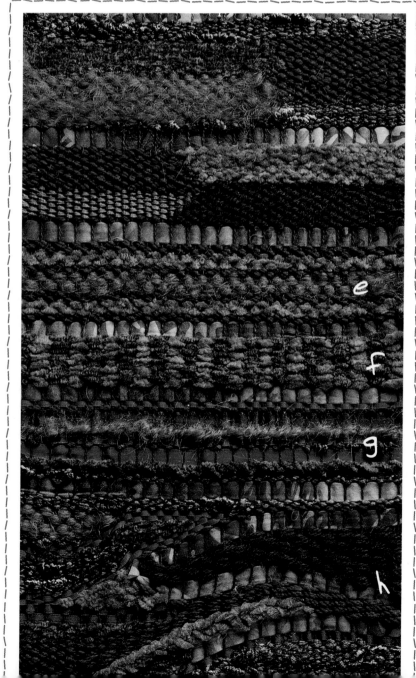

(continued)

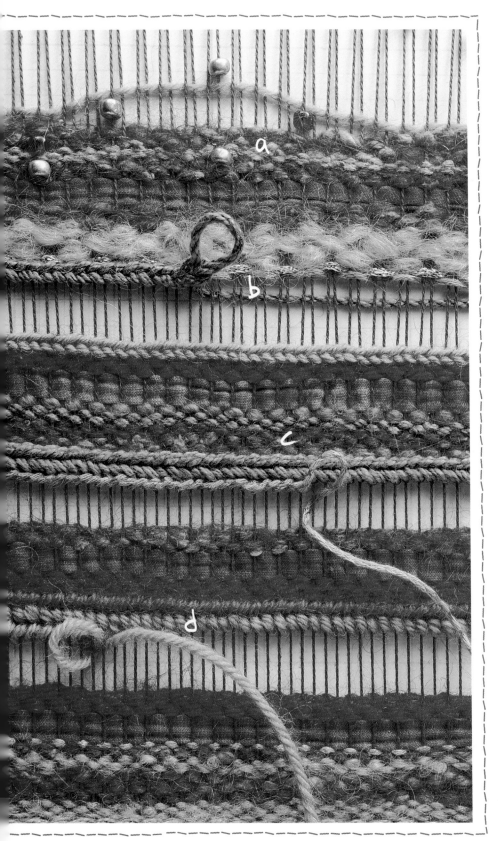

Weaving Design Details (continued)

Add beads (a) to warp yarns while stringing the warp, sliding beads to general locations. Work bead into position between weft materials; continue weaving around bead.

Chaining (b) is used to evenly separate and hold warp yarns apart. Run the weft under the warp from right to left. Form a small loop of weft to the left of the first warp yarn; bend it to the right, over the first warp. Reach through this loop and pull up a new loop of weft from under the warp. Bend new loop over to the right; tighten first loop. Continue across warp, chaining over each warp yarn in turn. After chaining over last warp yarn, pull weft through remaining loop to secure.

Soumak (c) is a technique of wrapping the weft around the warp to create textural interest. Draw the weft over the top of the first warp, down around it, then over it and the next warp, continuing across the warp in this forward over two, back under one pattern. After beating, the soumak forms a series of slightly sloping lines. By changing the direction of the slope on alternate wefts, you can create a herringbone or chevron pattern.

Egyptian knot (d) is an upside-down Soumak; work the weft forward under two warps and then back over one warp, and repeat across.

Oriental Soumak (e) is similar to Soumak. The weft is taken over four warps, back under two, forward over four, back under two, and so on.

Cavandoli knot (f) is made with the weft forming two half-hitch knots, one above the other, on one warp thread.

Greek knot (g) is a series of three half-hitches made one above the other on one warp yarn. Repeat it across as many warp yarns as desired to build a honeycomb of texture or use it alone for interest. Surround it with plain weave to make it more apparent.

Lark's head knot (h) is worked with individually cut yarns or fabric strips. Wrap the yarn under two warp yarns and then draw a loop of it up between the warps. Insert the ends through the loop and draw tight. When applying a series of lark's head knots, leave ends at random lengths for more interest.

RANDOM-CUT FABRIC WEAVING

Fabric artists often create "new cloth" from a collection of coordinating fabrics that are cut and pieced together. One method for creating this new cloth is called fabric weaving, in which fabric strips are interwoven and applied to a foundation. For visual interest, the strips are often cut with gently curving edges in varying widths. Random-cut fabric weaving allows you to use a variety of fabrics in both the warp and the weft, producing a new cloth with multiple colors, patterns, and visual textures.

The woven fabric strips are attached to a foundation of either fusible knit interfacing or a lightweight flannel. The raw edges of the strips, characteristic of fabric weaving, may be lightly secured with machine-guided or free-motion (page 88) stitching; additional decorative stitching may be used to create visual texture. Select fusible interfacing for the foundation if the intended purpose of the fabric is for a lightweight garment with a small amount of decorative stitching. If the fabric will be used for a heavier garment or if you intend to incorporate a lot of decorative stitching, select a flannel foundation.

Because garment pieces will be cut from your newly woven cloth, weave sections that are just large enough for each piece. Use a padded pinning board for your weaving surface; prepare small pieces on an ironing board. For ease of explanation in the directions that follow, the warp strips are cut beginning with the far left strip and working toward the right; the weft strips are cut from the top strip to the bottom strip. You may reverse the order or work from the center outward once you understand the technique.

MATERIALS

- Lightweight fabrics, in a variety of coordinating colors and prints; avoid fabrics that will ravel excessively.

- Rotary cutter and cutting mat.

- Padded pinning board, or foam-core board; pins.

- Fusible knit interfacing for foundation, if fabric will be used for lightweight garment with minimal decorative stitching.

- Lightweight cotton flannel for foundation, if woven fabric will be used for heavier garment or be heavily stitched.

- Masking tape, optional.

1 Cut a piece of desired foundation material slightly larger than dimensions of the pattern piece; smooth onto surface of pinning board. If using fusible knit interfacing, apply to the pinning board fusible side up. Secure foundation to board, pinning or taping around outer edges.

2 Sketch weave pattern, if desired, roughly planning size, shape, and number of strips necessary. Cut far left warp strip in desired width, length, and shape, using rotary cutter and mat.

3 Lap long right edge of first strip over second fabric. Cut second strip, using right edge of first strip as cutting guide for left edge and cutting right edge as desired.

4 Place first strip in position over foundation on pinning board; pin. Lap long right edge of second strip over third fabric. Cut third strip, using right edge of second strip as cutting guide for left edge and cutting right edge as desired.

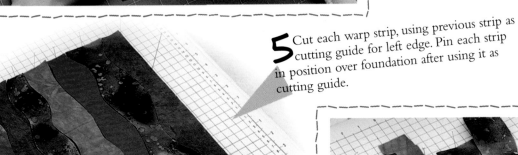

5 Cut each warp strip, using previous strip as cutting guide for left edge. Pin each strip in position over foundation after using it as cutting guide.

6 Cut weft strips, beginning with top strip and working toward bottom. Use lower edge of previous strip as cutting guide for upper edge of each strip. Weave weft strips through warp strips, aligning edges snugly while keeping strips flat; pin in position.

(continued)

7 **Fusible interfacing
foundation.** Cover
woven piece with press
cloth; press lightly to
partially fuse interfacing
to piece. Remove woven
piece from surface. Place
facedown on pressing
surface; press again to
completely fuse
interfacing.

7 **Flannel foundation.** Pin strips to
foundation around outer edge and
throughout piece. Remove woven piece
from surface. Baste around outer edge.
Stitch each strip to foundation, beginning
with center strips of warp and weft, and
working outward. Stitch near outer edges
on both sides of strips, or stitch wandering
lines through center of strips.

8 Add machine-guided or
free-motion decorative
stitches as desired.

Cut all warp strips from the same print fabric. Select progressively lighter colors for the weft strips, beginning with dark strips at the top.

Cut strips more narrow through the center of the piece, widening them toward the outer edges.

Experiment with different weave patterns, such as this basket weave (over two, under one).

QUILTED EFFECTS

Many fabric artists include some form of quilting in their projects, whether these are made from pieced fabric or whole cloth. Quilting adds wonderful texture and dimension, a feast for the eyes as well as the fingertips. Decorative threads, double-needle stitching (page 87), and even decorative bobbin thread sewing (page 84) may be used for special effects. The challenge in successful apparel quilting is to acquire the desired appearance without forfeiting the drapable quality of the fabric. Ideally, a quilted garment is comfortable and soft, molding to the body's form rather than holding a stiff shape of its own. The fabrics and battings selected as well as the density and style of quilting stitches all affect the final appearance and drape of the garment.

ᨆᨆᨆ Quilting Basics

The possibilities for quilted effects are seemingly endless. Some techniques are machine-guided, meaning the feed dogs and presser foot guide the fabric. An Even Feed® foot is useful for feeding fabric and batting layers evenly to prevent puckers, though for some intricate work, an open-toe embroidery foot allows better visibility. While machine-guided quilting is helpful for some effects, such as marked gridwork **(a),** you may find it cumbersome and limiting for effects like echo quilting **(b)** or small-scale background quilting **(c),** techniques that require frequent directional changes. In free-motion quilting, the layers are guided by hand, allowing you to stitch in any direction without turning the fabric and to stitch tight corners and intricate curves with ease.

Garment quilting often consists of repetitive lines or designs filling in areas for backgound texture. Many geometric quilting patterns (left) used by fabric artists are based on the Japanese Sashiko style of quilting, in which a gridwork of repetitive designs is completed by stitching in a continuous line, following an efficient, predetermined path. Try some of the examples shown here or on pages 60 and 61, or work out unique patterns of your own on graph paper, charting efficient stitch paths. Mark the pattern on your fabric, and stitch the designs in either machine-guided or free-motion quilting.

Whenever possible, complete the quilting before cutting garment pieces to size, as the quilting process will shrink the size of the fabric. This also gives you excess fabric to grasp when you are doing free-motion quilting. For garments with shoulder seams, cut the front and back pieces with generous seam and hem allowances on all but the shoulder seam. Join the pieces at the shoulder before layering and quilting, minimizing bulk and allowing you to quilt in a continuous pattern from the front to the back.

⌇⌇⌇⌇ Batting

One of the keys to creating drapable quilted fabric is selecting the appropriate batting. Many low-loft and extra-low-loft battings are available, including those with fiber contents of cotton, polyester, cotton/polyester blend, and wool. Each of these fibers has characteristics that determine the batting's suitability for your project. Cotton battings are very soft, drapable, and breathable for lightweight garments. They may tend to separate or bunch easily and must therefore be quilted with no more than 2" to 3" (5 to 7.5 cm) spaces between stitches. Polyester is more stable, so the quilting lines can be farther apart, but fiber ends may tend to *beard*, or penetrate through to the surface of the fabric. Blended battings take advantage of the positive characteristics of both fibers. Wool batting is soft, warm, and resilient, and has firmer body than cotton or polyester. *Needlepunching* is a process that gives the batting firmer body to resist separation or bunching, allowing you to quilt with larger spaces between stitching lines. While this is desirable for larger quilts and crafting or home decorating projects, it may be too firm for a garment. For shrinkage control, natural-fiber battings should be prewashed, following the manufacturer's directions. However, some artists prefer to quilt the fabric with unwashed batting and then wash and dry the quilted piece before cutting out garment sections. This produces a deeper "dimpling" of the surface. For a thinner look, batting may also be split in half, though if you intend to prewash the batting, split it after washing and drying. Cotton flannel fabric is another useful alternative to batting when a thin appearance is desired. Due to its high rate of shrinkage, cotton flannel should always be prewashed.

⌇⌇⌇⌇ Fabric

The fabric selected will naturally play a major role in the final drapability and appearance of the quilted garment. Lightweight to mediumweight closely woven natural-fiber fabrics produce the best results, with softly dimpled texture. Fine-quality pure cotton fabric is easiest to work with and the most widely used. Silk fabrics, including broadcloth, noile, dupioni, and crepe-de-chine produce luxurious quilted effects. Frequent needle changes may be necessary for extensive sewing on silk because the filament may dull the needle and

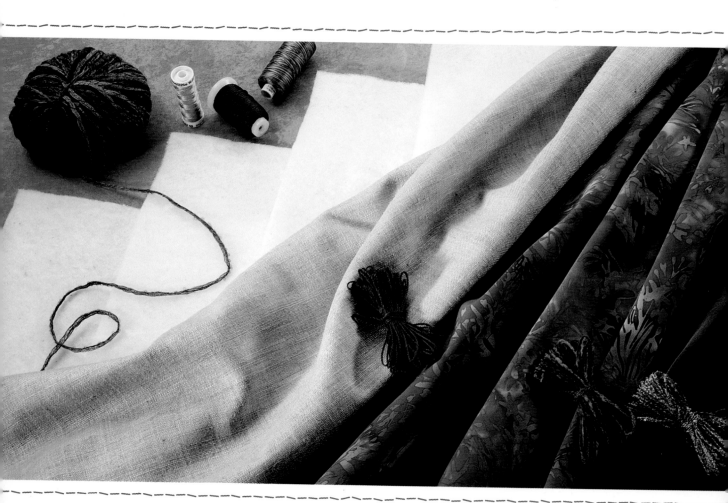

Experiment with various battings, fabrics, yarns, and threads to develop a combination with your preferred drapability, texture, and artistic appeal.

cause skipped stitches. Rayon is soft and drapes well, but like some silks, it is slippery and shifts easily during construction. Linen is characteristically crisp; you may want to wash and dry it several times for a softer quilted look. Washing any fabric before quilting will help to eliminate skipped stitches.

Select lightweight backing fabric with the same qualities as the outer fabric, especially if the project is intended to be reversible. If your outer fabric is a solid color, consider using a print backing fabric and motif-quilting from the backing side, thus "sketching" the print onto the outer fabric in quilting stitches.

∿∿∿ Threads

Select threads according to the effect you want to create. Invisible nylon thread works well when quilted background texture is your goal. It is also useful when quilting multicolored or pieced fabric, as it blends easily from one color to the next. Select cotton or polyester thread in a color to match or coordinate with the fabric when you want the quilting stitches to be

more visible, yet subtle. Decorative threads draw attention, making them the primary focus over the quilted texture. Rayon and cotton embroidery threads and some metallic threads can be threaded through the machine needle and sewn on the right side. Though some heavier decorative threads will fit through the eye of a larger needle, consider sewing with the decorative thread in the bobbin (page 84). This allows you to use a smaller machine needle, resulting in better quality quilting stitches. Couching (page 80) is another technique that can be used to simultaneously quilt and embellish the fabric.

Always make a test sample, 12" to 15" (30.5 to 38 cm) square, using the desired batting, outer fabric, and backing fabric. Divide the sample into sections, quilting areas with varying densities and stitch styles. This is a good time to try some new techniques, such as couching or decorative bobbin thread stitching, or to practice free-motion sewing skills. Measure your sample after quilting; then wash and dry it. Measure it again, and evaluate the piece for loft, size, texture or smoothness, drapability or stiffness, and the condition of the batting in unstitched areas.

∿∿how_to Prepare Fabric for Quilting ∿∿∿∿∿∿∿∿∿∿∿∿∿∿∿∿∿∿∿∿

2 Place backing fabric facedown on work surface; place batting over backing fabric. Place garment fabric faceup over batting. Baste layers together, using grid of hand basting or safety pins, spaced about 3" (7.5 cm) apart. Closer basting lines may be necessary if fabric is slippery or if you will not be using an Even Feed® presser foot.

1 Preshrink outer fabric and backing fabric, if necessary. Wash and dry batting, if desired, following manufacturer's directions. Split batting, if desired. Mark design or guidelines (page 104) on right side of outer fabric if quilting will be done from outside; mark on right side of backing fabric if quilting will be done from backing side.

Tips for Machine-guided Quilting

Attach Even Feed® presser foot or walking foot for strip quilting **(a)** or straight-line stitching. Set machine for a straight stitch with 10 to 12 stitches per inch (2.5 cm).

Attach open-toe embroidery foot for intricate machine-guided quilting stitches that require more visibility **(b).**

Position hands on either side of presser foot. Gently press down and hold fabric taut to prevent layers from shifting, causing puckers or tucks. Ease any excess fabric under the presser foot as you stitch.

Begin and end stitching lines with 8 to 10 very short stitches to secure threads.

Stitch-in-the-ditch quilting. Stitch over seamlines in pieced fabric, stitching in the well of the seams.

Channel quilting. Stitch a series of relatively parallel lines. To create more interest, lines need not be evenly spaced.

Ideas for Machine-guided Background Quilting

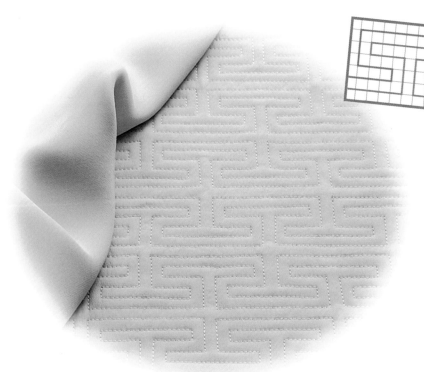

First stitch the green lines throughout the entire piece. Then stitch the pink lines.

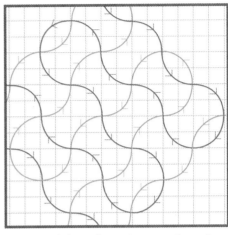

First stitch lines shown in green throughout entire piece. Then stitch lines shown in pink, stitching across previous stitches.

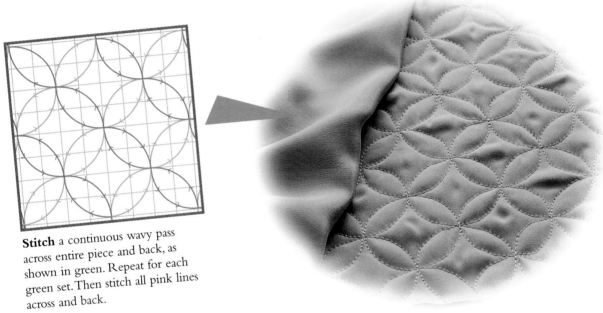

Stitch a continuous wavy pass across entire piece and back, as shown in green. Repeat for each green set. Then stitch all pink lines across and back.

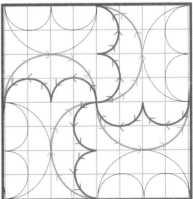

Stitch wide arcs throughout entire piece, as indicated in green. Then stitch all narrower arcs, as indicated in pink.

Set machine for straight stitch. Attach darning foot. Lower or cover feed dogs. If neither option is possible with your machine, set stitch length at 0.

Lower the presser foot. This is not always obvious when using a darning foot.

Position hands so they act as a hoop, encircling needle. Gently press down and pull outward to create tension on fabric. Move fabric with wrist and hand movements as you stitch. Rest elbows comfortably on sewing table while stitching; it may be helpful to elevate elbows on books. Wear rubber fingertip covers for more control.

Begin and end stitching lines with 8 to 10 very short stitches to secure threads.

Maintain steady rhythm and speed as you stitch to keep the stitch length uniform.

Motif quilting. Outline desired motifs in a print; stitch from one motif to another with continuous stitches.

Marked-design quilting. Outline design first. Then stitch inner design lines, moving continuously from one area to another.

Echo quilting. Outline a central motif or design. Stitch evenly spaced lines, moving outward from the motif or design.

Continuous-line background quilting. Any pattern that can be drawn on paper without lifting the pencil can also be stitched without stopping. These lines are often stitched around a motif, appliqué, or trapunto design to make it more apparent.

Curvy lines and loops of the butterfly motif are repeated continuously in the background quilting.

Alternating parallel stitching lines fill an area with a square grid design.

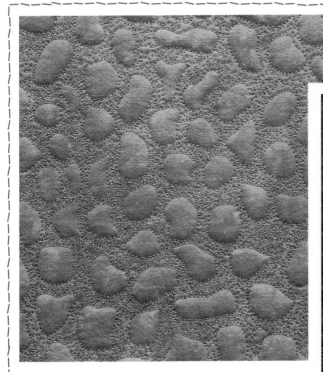

Wavy lines resemble rippling water.

Outlined shapes become more pronounced when separated with stippling stitches.

TRAPUNTO

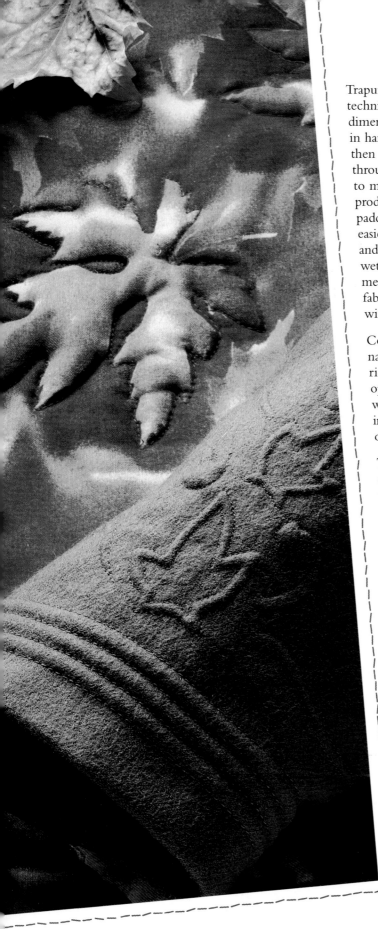

Trapunto, also known as *Italian quilting,* is a versatile quilting technique that raises the elements of a design for a three-dimensional effect. Traditionally, design shapes were outlined in hand stitching through two layers of fabric. Tiny slits were then cut into the backing fabric and stuffing was inserted through the holes to pad the shapes. Trapunto adapts well to machine sewing, which speeds up the process and produces impressive results. Using this method, shapes are padded with batting as they are stitched, a technique made easier by innovative sewing notions, like wash-away thread and water-soluble marking pens. Because the fabric must be wetted to remove wash-away thread and marking pen, this method for padded designs is only suitable for washable fabric or fabric that will not be damaged by spraying it with water.

Corded quilting is another style of trapunto in which narrow stitched channels are filled with yarn to create ridges. This makes a subtle, but effective, accent along front opening edges or hems. Padded designs and corded quilting work well together or can be used alone. Additional quilting (page 56) can be worked between corded quilting rows or around padded designs to enhance them.

The shadows and highlights of trapunto's dimensional effects are more apparent when worked on solid-color fabrics. Finely woven natural-fiber fabrics, including cotton, wool, and silk, work well. Linen can be softened first by washing and tumbling dry. Synthetic fabrics may tend to pucker around the padded areas more than natural fabrics. Prints tend to obscure the design, and your work will be in vain. However, trapunto can be used to emphasize and give dimension to a portion of a print, such as a distinct floral motif. Any method of trapunto will alter the size of the fabric, so it is important to preshrink the fabric and complete the trapunto before cutting out pattern pieces.

Work a test sample to determine the machine settings for free-motion stitching, the width of stitched channels, and the number of yarn strands necessary for corded quilting. Underfilled channels are not as visually effective; overfilled channels may produce puckers or stiffness.

M A T E R I A L S

◆ Outer fabric.

◆ Backing fabric.

◆ Lightweight fusible interfacing, optional.

◆ High-loft batting; low-loft batting.

◆ Acrylic baby yarn and yarn needle.

◆ Wash-away thread.

◆ Fabric marker.

◆ Stylus.

2 Thread machine with wash-away thread; use regular sewing thread in the bobbin. Attach presser foot, and adjust machine for desired technique. Stitch on outer design lines.

1 Transfer design (page 104) to right side of outer fabric. Pin high-loft batting to wrong side of fabric; baste or secure with safety pins.

3 Trim away batting in areas that are to appear flat, using blunt-end scissors and trimming close to stitching line.

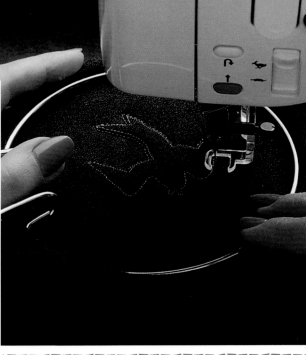

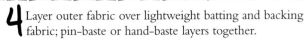

4 Layer outer fabric over lightweight batting and backing fabric; pin-baste or hand-baste layers together.

5 Thread machine with regular sewing thread or decorative thread. Stitch around design, stitching close to previous stitches; stitch any interior design lines. Fill in flat areas around padded design with quilting stitches (page 56), if desired.

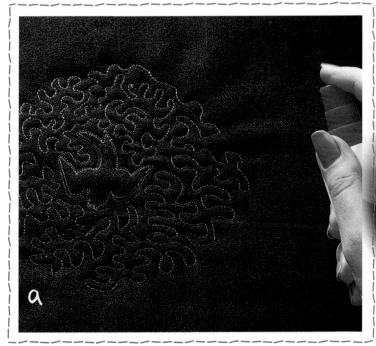

a

6 Spray nonwashable quilted fabric (a) with cool water to remove wash-away thread. Or immerse washable quilted fabric (b) in cool water one to two minutes to dissolve wash-away thread and remove water-soluble marker lines, if used. Dry flat, or tumble dry to create more texture.

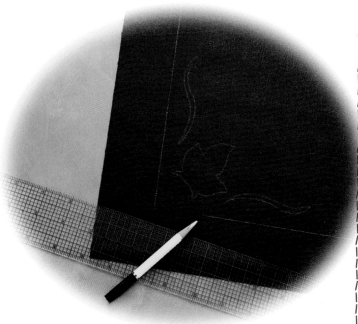

1 Preshrink outer fabric, backing fabric, and any interfacing. Apply interfacing, if desired, following manufacturer's directions. Transfer design (page 104) to right side of fabric. For continuous rows, mark first row; use presser foot as guide for additional rows.

2 Pin outer fabric to backing fabric, wrong sides together; baste. Stitch design lines, using embroidery foot or Even Feed® foot.

3 Thread yarn needle with several strands of yarn (number determined in test sample) cut to full length of channel. Insert yarn into channel.

4 Bring needle through backing fabric at corner; trim yarn.

5 Repeat steps 3 and 4, filling all channels. Poke yarn ends under backing fabric, using stylus. Place completed fabric facedown on padded pressing surface; press lightly.

Shallow

pleats add textural interest to your sewing project. They can be used for cuffs, collars, pockets, or inserts on garments. Pillows, placemats, and cornice boards may be enhanced with pleated fabric. A cloth pleater, designed for making perfectly spaced pleats, allows you to pleat the fabric before cutting your pattern, and eliminates the need for tedious marking and basting. By skipping slots in the pleater, you can vary the size and spacing of the pleats. The pleats can be held in place permanently with fusible interfacing, decorative topstitching, or couching, if desired.

Many fabrics are suitable for pleated effects. Best results are achieved with lightweight to mediumweight fabrics. Depending on the pleat design, the process may require fabric two to three times the size of the finished piece. Pleats made in 100% polyester fabric can be permanently set by using a press cloth and an iron set at a high temperature. This is especially suitable for

PLEATED EFFECTS

edgings and any other pleated accents that are not held in place by decorative stitching or fusing.

Use of the pleater does not limit you to perfect, evenly spaced pleats. Many interesting variations can be developed. Experiment with irregular pleating and even create erratic, free-form effects. Change the grainline in any direction you choose. Turn pleats in opposite directions from each other. Create irregular folds or run a crosswise fold through the fabric before pleating. Once you begin to experiment, you will find there are no restrictions to your pleating creativity.

MATERIALS

- Cloth pleater, such as EZE Pleater™ or Perfect Pleater™.
- Lightweight to mediumweight fabric.
- Lightweight fusible interfacing.
- Decorative thread for topstitching or couching.

1 Position pleater on pressing surface with folds facing away from you. Place fabric facedown over pleater, allowing edge nearest you to extend at least ⅝" (1.5 cm) off pleater, for seam allowance.

2 Tuck fabric behind cloth-covered louver, using fingers or point turner. Repeat until three or four pleats have been formed. Press with steam iron.

3 Repeat step 2 until desired length has been pleated. Allow enough excess unpleated fabric for seaming.

4 Cover pleated fabric with damp press cloth; set iron at high temperature. Press entire piece until press cloth is dry, to set pleats **(a)**. Or place fusible interfacing, fusible side down, over pleated fabric; fuse, following manufacturer's directions, to lock pleats **(b)**.

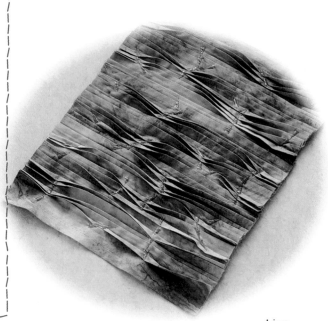

5 Allow fabric to cool. Roll pleater back to release fabric. Place pleated fabric, right side up, on pressing surface; press again to sharpen folds.

6 Embellish pleated fabric with decorative machine stitching or couching, if desired.

how_to Join Pleated Panels

1 Lap one panel over the next so pleats form continuous pattern. Pin folded edge of lapped pleat through all layers.

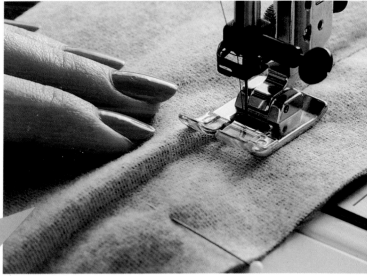

2 Turn pinned fabric facedown; pin seam allowances together. Stitch and finish.

TEXTURIZING FABRICS

Smooth fabrics can be texturized to give them more visual and tactile appeal. Sections of texturized fabric can be incorporated into a pieced cloth to create an interesting wall hanging or pillow front. Or they can become an intriguing design element in an artistic garment.

Some methods of texturizing, such as bubbling and crinkling, require that you first manipulate the fabric in some way to create the texture. The texture is then permanently retained by fusing interfacing to the wrong side of the fabric.

To texturize by shrinking, select two natural fabrics that will shrink when they are washed but will not be damaged by hot water. Cotton, linen, rayon, and some silks will work well for the outer fabric. If the foundation fabric will show, you can use the same or similar fabric; otherwise, simple cotton muslin will work. The outer fabric is preshrunk; the foundation fabric is not. Once the two fabrics are sewn together, washing and drying them causes the foundation to shrink, thus puckering the outer fabric.

Consider the final use for the texturized fabric when you are preparing it. It is easier to work with small pieces rather than one large one, if your project will permit.

how to Bubble Fabric

MATERIALS

- Fabric.
- Raised metal grid, such as kitchen cooling rack; pencil with rubber eraser.
- Lightweight fusible knit interfacing.

1 Cut 18" (46 cm) square of fabric. Wet fabric thoroughly; squeeze out excess moisture. Place damp fabric, right side down, over slightly raised metal grid, such as kitchen cooling rack.

2 Poke fabric down ½" (1.3 cm) into each hole of grid, using eraser end of pencil; begin at center and work outward, controlling fabric with fingers. Fabric will shrink up to about half its size.

(continued)

3 Cut fusible interfacing to same size as bubbled fabric; place, fusible side down, over bubbled fabric. Press interfacing to fuse while fabric is still in grid. Allow fabric to dry thoroughly.

4 Gently remove fabric from grid. Embellish with decorative stitching, if desired.

~~~ how_to Crinkle Fabric ~~~~~~~~~~~~~~~~~~~~~~~~~~~~~~~

M A T E R I A L S

• Fabric, preferably natural.

• Cotton string or thick rubber bands; hosiery.

• Washer and dryer.

• Lightweight fusible interfacing.

1 Wet fabric thoroughly in lukewarm water; squeeze out excess moisture. Place fabric flat on work surface. Gather fabric with fingers along lengthwise grain, forming narrow roll.

2 Twist ends of roll in opposite directions, squeezing out any bubbles that form while twisting; continue twisting until fabric is twisted as tight as possible and begins to curl.

3 Fold twisted roll in half, if necessary. Continue twisting, allowing fabric to curl into small, twisted ball.

4 Tie ball with cotton string or secure with thick rubber bands. Tie ball into toe of hosiery. Dry fabric in clothes dryer with towels; towels absorb moisture and help reduce noise. Depending on amount of fabric, this step could take several hours.

(continued)

5 Unroll dry fabric gently; place, right side down, on pressing surface. Spread fabric to desired width, smoothing crinkles to desired texture.

6 Place fusible interfacing, fusible side down, over crinkled fabric. Fuse interfacing, following manufacturer's directions.

MATERIALS

◆ Natural fabric, such as cotton, linen, rayon, or silk, for outer fabric.

◆ Untreated natural fabric, such as 78/76 muslin or cotton flannel, for foundation fabric.

◆ Washer and dryer.

1 Wash outer fabric in warm water; machine dry. Press. Do not preshrink foundation fabric. Place outer fabric over foundation fabric, wrong sides together; pin around outer edges and throughout interior.

2 Stitch fabric to foundation, following desired grid pattern, such as squares or diamonds. Stitching lines may be wavy or straight; spaces between lines should be no more than 1½" to 2" (3.8 to 5 cm) wide.

3 Wash stitched fabric in very hot water; machine dry. Foundation fabric will shrink, causing outer fabric to ripple and pucker.

COUCHING

Apply decorative cords, yarns, and ribbons to the fabric surface by couching. Arrange the trim on the fabric surface, following marked design lines, and stitch over it, using one of several stitch options. Use monofilament thread and a blindstitch or simple zigzag pattern for nearly invisible stitches, allowing the decorative cords to seemingly float on the surface of the fabric. If you want to incorporate the machine thread into the overall effect, use regular sewing thread or decorative thread in the desired color and stitch over the trim, using a zigzag, multiple zigzag, or decorative stitch pattern. Experiment with various decorative stitches to get the look you want. Some flat trims and ribbons can be couched onto the surface, using a double needle (page 87) and a decorative machine stitch.

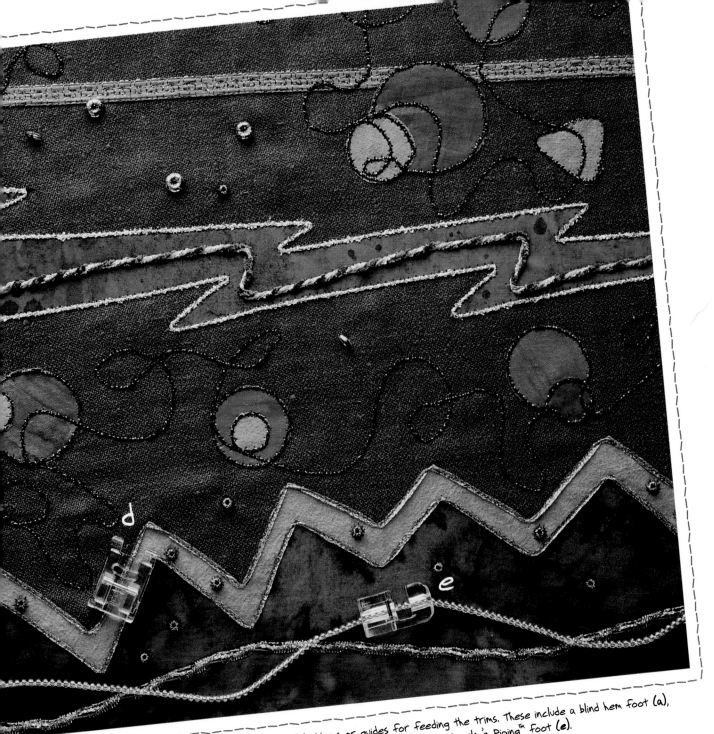

Presser feet suitable for couching feature recessed bottoms or guides for feeding the trims. These include a blind hem foot (a), an Open-toe embroidery foot (b), a cording foot (c), a buttonhole foot (d), and a Pearls 'n Piping™ foot (e).

Couch trims ¼" (6 mm) or narrower, using an open-toe embroidery foot. Apply very small trims with a cording foot, freeing your hands to guide the fabric while the foot guides the trim. A blind hem foot or other specialty presser foot may also be used. Stabilize (page 108) lightweight or mediumweight fabric with fusible interfacing or removable stabilizer. It is usually not necessary to stabilize heavy fabrics or quilted fabrics.

Whenever possible, cut the decorative trim to the desired length plus additional length for finishing. Couching trims directly off a spool or skein creates extra tension and may cause puckering. As with any other technique, it is important to practice on a sample of the fabric to determine stitch settings and the easiest method for guiding the trim.

1 Attach desired presser foot to machine. Thread machine with desired sewing thread or decorative thread; wind bobbin with lightweight thread. Apply stabilizer under fabric, if desired. Cut trim to desired length plus 8" to 10" (20.5 to 25.5 cm). Insert trim through hole in presser foot or position trim under foot with 4" (10 cm) excess behind foot.

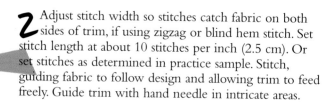

2 Adjust stitch width so stitches catch fabric on both sides of trim, if using zigzag or blind hem stitch. Set stitch length at about 10 stitches per inch (2.5 cm). Or set stitches as determined in practice sample. Stitch, guiding fabric to follow design and allowing trim to feed freely. Guide trim with hand needle in intricate areas.

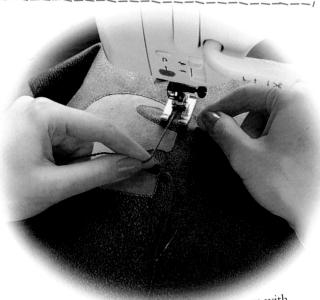

3 Ease trim around curves. Turn sharp corners with needle down in fabric on same side of trim as direction of turn.

4 Secure threads at beginning and end of stitching line by pulling to back side and knotting. Secure ends of couched trim as shown opposite. Remove stabilizer and markings as necessary. Press lightly from back side, taking care not to flatten trim.

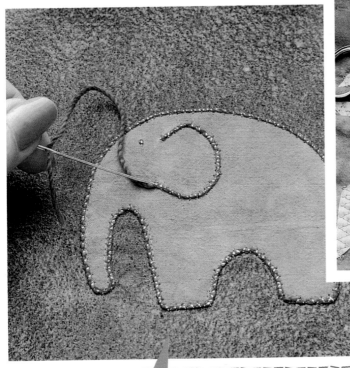

Apply liquid fray preventer to wide trim at end of stitching line; allow to dry. Trim even with end of stitching line.

Thread end of narrow cord or yarn through tapestry needle, and stitch to wrong side; knot together with bobbin and top threads on wrong side. Clip trim, leaving short tail.

Enclose end of trim in seamline whenever possible. Or cover end with appliqué.

Knot multiple cord ends together at end of stitching line; allow to fray or hang freely for decorative effect.

DECORATIVE BOBBIN THREAD SEWING

Decorative threads too thick to thread through the eye of the sewing machine needle can be wound on the bobbin and stitched onto the surface from the wrong side of the fabric. Because the stitching is done facedown, even the artist must wait to view the results. Exquisite designs can be created using metallic threads, pearl cotton, pearl rayon, ribbon threads, or embroidery floss. The stitching may follow a marked design **(a)**, using machine-guided stitching or using free-motion techniques. For a free-form effect, areas can be stitched with free-motion random stippling **(b)** or decorated more heavily with free-motion fill-in stitches **(c)**. Rows of decorative stitch patterns or utility stitch patterns **(d)** can be used to create attractive edgings or borders.

Experimentation is the key to success in decorative bobbin thread stitching. A few basic guidelines and a little practice will help you eliminate the guesswork in achieving the look you want. Begin experimenting with straight stitches. Generally, the character of the

decorative threads and cords is better defined when the machine stitch length is set at eight to ten stitches per inch (2.5 cm). Enlarge decorative stitch patterns and utility stitch patterns whenever possible for a more pronounced look. Try various threads and cords in your bobbin to see which ones produce the desired results. Follow your sewing machine manufacturer's instructions for adjusting or bypassing bobbin thread tension. Thread the sewing machine needle with invisible nylon thread or regular sewing thread in a color to match the background fabric. Adjust needle thread tension, if necessary, to produce the desired quality of stitches on the decorative side.

Wind decorative threads onto wind-in-place bobbins by hand, using firm, even tension and winding in the same direction as the bobbin would be wound on the machine. Wind other bobbins on the machine at slow speed, bypassing tension discs. Hold a large or awkward spool on a pencil or place it in a jar on the floor, controlling thread tension with the fingers.

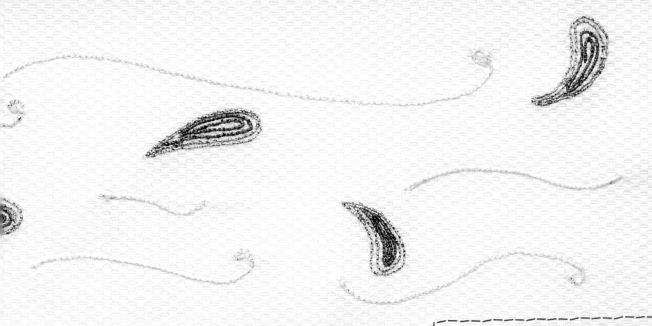

Tips for Sewing with Decorative Bobbin Thread

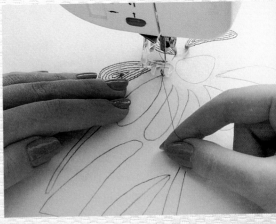

Mark design guide-lines on stabilizer; for asymmetrical designs, mark mirror image. Press freezer paper, shiny side down, to wrong side of fabric. Or baste tear-away stabilizer to wrong side of fabric. Or fuse interfacing to wrong side of the fabric.

Bring bobbin thread to wrong side at beginning and end of stitching; knot top and bobbin threads together. Trim, leaving short tails if sewing single layer. If sewing through multiple layers, thread tails through tapestry needle and hide them between layers. Avoid backstitching or stitching in place.

Attach darning presser foot for free-motion stitching. (Front of foot has been cut away for better visibility.) Lower or cover feed dogs, or adjust stitch length to 0, if feed dogs cannot be lowered or covered.

Attach open-toe presser foot for sewing utility patterns, decorative patterns, straight-line stitching, or any machine-guided designs.

DOUBLE-NEEDLE STITCHING

Give your fabric added dimension and design interest with double-needle stitching. Using decorative threads, stitch over texturized or pleated fabric with scattered rows of double-needle stitching. Stitch quilted effects, using a double needle to give the fabric a distinctive character. Create depth and texture with meandering trails of wide double-needle stitching, forming ridges over the fabric.

Double-needle labeling indicates the space between the needles, followed by the needle size. The range suitable for most machines includes needles from 1.6 mm/80 to 6.0 mm/100.

Widely separated double needles are suitable for straight stitching. Narrower double needles can be used with some decorative machine stitches, provided the width of the stitch allows the needles to clear the throat plate and presser foot openings. Always test the stitches carefully, turning the handwheel to avoid breaking the needles or damaging the machine.

Tips for Double-needle Stitching

Pull needle threads through to the wrong side at beginning and end of stitching lines; tie off securely with bobbin thread.

Use an embroidery foot for straight or decorative stitches that lie flat on the surface of the fabric; use a pintuck foot when stitching parallel rows of ridges.

Tighten bobbin tension slightly or use heavier thread in the bobbin, to create a more pronounced ridge on right side of the fabric. Tighten needle tension slightly if no ridge is desired.

Stabilize wrong side of lightweight or stretchy fabrics with fusible knit interfacing or freezer paper, for better stitch quality.

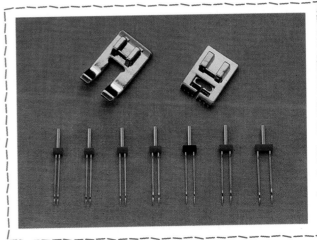

Cutout bottom of open-toe embroidery foot rides over ridges or decorative stitches. Pintuck feet have several cutout slots; select double needles to match slot widths.

FREE-MOTION MACHINE STITCHING

Free-motion stitching is used extensively by fabric artists in various techniques to create interesting surface designs and textures. With free-motion stitching, the artist uses the sewing machine needle to create colorful thread designs on fabric in much the same way that one would use a pencil to draw on paper. The difference is, of course, that you move the "paper" instead of the "pencil." In free-motion stitching, the presser foot is removed, or, in some cases, a darning foot is used. The feed dogs are covered or lowered, if possible, and the stitch length and direction are controlled by the artist moving the fabric around over the bed of the machine. Straight stitches are generally used for thread sketching, when you want to outline a design or trail colorful thread lines over the fabric. Many quilted effects (page 56) employ free-motion thread sketching, as do some styles of decorative bobbin thread stitching (page 84).

When free-motion stitching a single layer of fabric, you must stabilize the fabric (page 108) in some way to prevent it from puckering. Most often, the fabric is held taut in an embroidery hoop. A wooden hoop with a fixing screw works best because it can be tightened firmly. Select a hoop that

is ¼" (6 mm) thick so that it can be easily slid under the machine needle. Depending on the fabric weight and stitch style, you may need to stabilize the fabric further, using one of the products or methods on pages 108 and 109.

Machine embroidery threads, available in cotton, rayon, and metallics, provide the best results. They range from 30-weight to 60-weight, with the lower number being the heavier thread. Use a sharp, new needle in a size large enough to prevent the threads from splitting or shredding. For sewing with cotton embroidery thread, use a fine needle in size 70/9 or 80/11. Use a size 80/11 or 90/14 with rayon and metallic threads. Specialty needles, such as the Metalfil® needle by Lamertz, are designed to produce optimum stitch quality with rayon and metallic threads. For most purposes, cotton basting thread or fine monofilament nylon thread may be used in the bobbin. It may be necessary to adjust the thread tension so the bobbin thread does not show on the right side of the fabric.

1 Wrap inner ring of wooden embroidery hoop with cotton twill tape to protect delicate fabrics and prevent fabric from loosening while stitching. Secure ends with fabric glue.

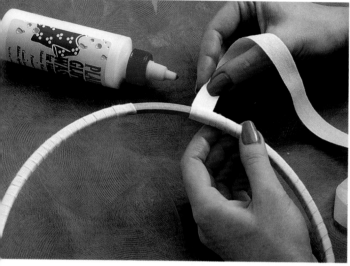

2 Mark design on right side of fabric or on water-soluble stabilizer pinned to surface of fabric, if desired. Loosen fixing screw slightly; separate rings. Place fabric over outer ring, right side up, centering design.

3 Push inner ring into outer ring with heels of palms, keeping fabric taut. Partially tighten screw; gently pull fabric edges evenly until fabric is very taut. Take care not to distort the grainline.

4 Push inner ring to underside about ⅛" (3 mm); this helps to tighten fabric and helps fabric slide smoothly over machine bed. Tighten screw with screwdriver.

Place tear-away stabilizer under fabric before stitching.

Lower presser foot lever, engaging tension discs. This is not always apparent when sewing without presser foot or with darning foot. Stitch in place a few times to secure stitches at beginning and end or whenever changing colors.

Relax. Sit directly in front of needle. Rest hands comfortably on sides of hoop; do not grip hoop. Guide fabric with wrist motions, resting elbows on table or on books stacked around bed of machine, so shoulders are not tense.

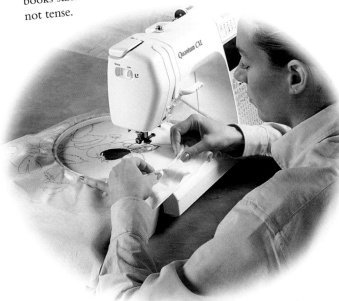

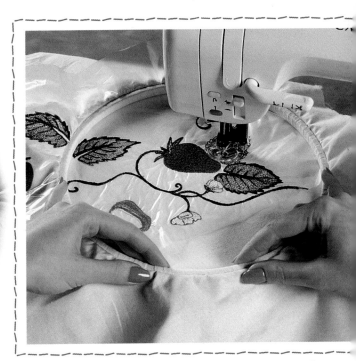

Practice. Develop a rhythm, moving the fabric at a smooth, even pace. Run machine at moderate to fast speed, moving hoop slowly as you stitch, to obtain desired stitch length.

MACHINE OPENWORK

Create intriguing designs with machine openwork. Layered over contrasting fabric, openwork invites a peek into the "hidden" underlayer. Or openwork can be used alone to give a lacy effect to the fabric. For best results, select a closely woven fabric that does not ravel excessively, or stabilize ravelly fabric with lightweight knit interfacing. Cut out simple shapes, such as irregular circles, ovals, or freeforms. Set your machine for free-motion stitching as on page 88. Attach a darning foot, and thread the machine with the same thread in the needle and bobbin; decorative threads work well for this technique. Check your machine for balanced tension. Because you will be constantly rotating the hoop, it is easiest to work this technique on relatively small pieces of fabric.

M A T E R I A L S

- ◆ Fabric.
- ◆ Lightweight fusible knit interfacing, optional.
- ◆ Fine decorative threads, suitable for both needle and bobbin.
- ◆ Wooden embroidery hoop.
- ◆ Darning foot.

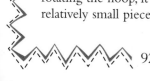

1 Fuse lightweight knit interfacing to wrong side of fabric, if fabric tends to ravel. On right side, draw outlines of openings, using removable marker or fine chalk line. Place fabric in hoop (page 90), stretching fabric taut.

2 Prepare machine as described opposite. Slide hooped fabric under darning foot. Stitch free-motion straight stitch three times around each marked outline, stitching over previous stitches with each pass.

3 Remove hooped fabric from machine. Cut out inside of one shape, using small sharp-pointed scissors. Cut as close as possible to stitches.

4 Slide hooped fabric back under darning foot. Stitch in place for a few stitches at top edge of stitched shape.

(continued)

5 Stitch across opening to opposite side, stitching at medium speed. Move hoop smoothly and steadily. Stitch just past outline stitches.

6 Stitch along outside edge of shape to another point; turn hoop so you will be stitching toward yourself.

Stitch Pattern Ideas ~~~~~~~~~~~~~~~~~~~~~~~~~~~~

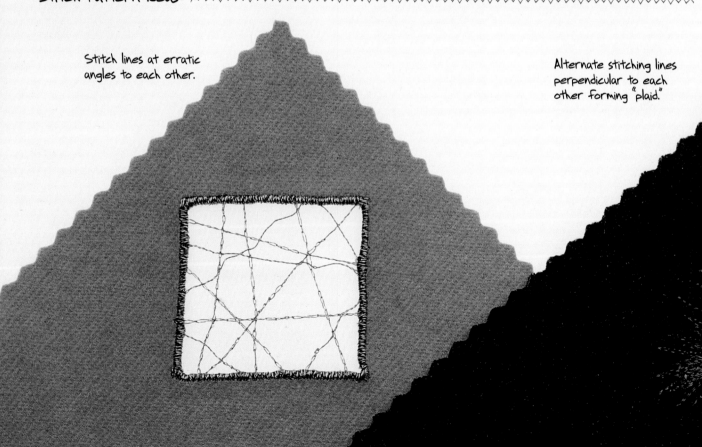

Stitch lines at erratic angles to each other.

Alternate stitching lines perpendicular to each other forming "plaid."

7 Repeat steps 5 and 6 until opening has been filled with desired amount of stitching lines, in desired pattern. Finish outer edge of shape with free-motion stitching or machine-guided decorative stitching in desired pattern.

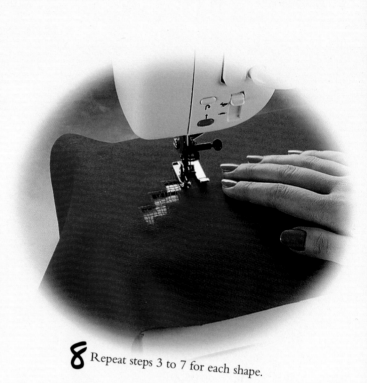

8 Repeat steps 3 to 7 for each shape.

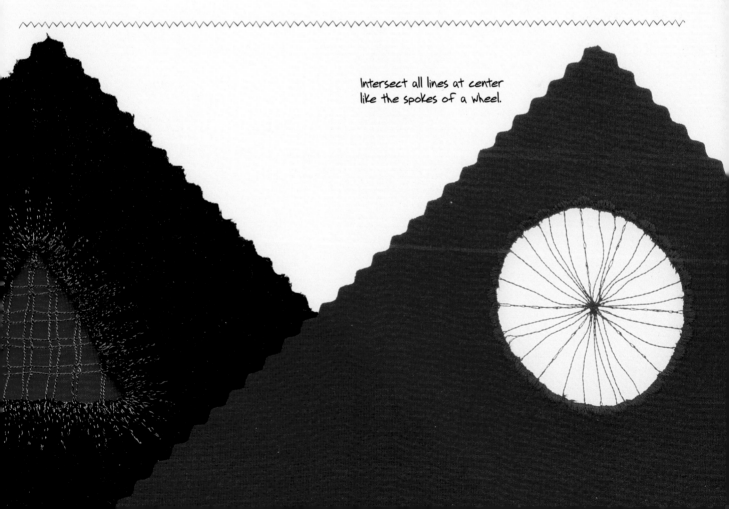

Intersect all lines at center like the spokes of a wheel.

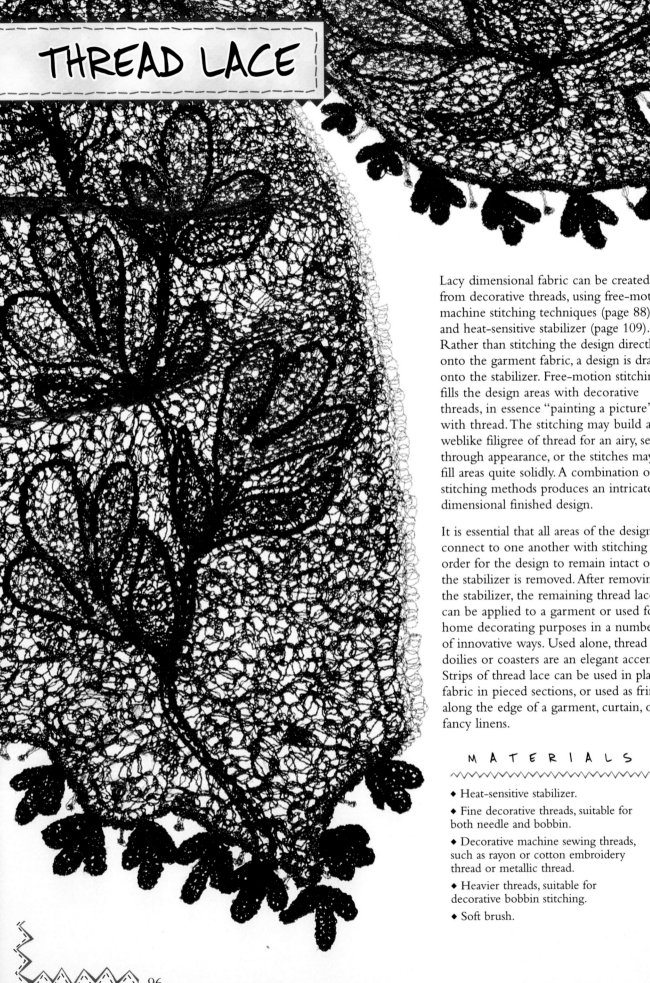

THREAD LACE

Lacy dimensional fabric can be created from decorative threads, using free-motion machine stitching techniques (page 88) and heat-sensitive stabilizer (page 109). Rather than stitching the design directly onto the garment fabric, a design is drawn onto the stabilizer. Free-motion stitching fills the design areas with decorative threads, in essence "painting a picture" with thread. The stitching may build a weblike filigree of thread for an airy, see-through appearance, or the stitches may fill areas quite solidly. A combination of stitching methods produces an intricate, dimensional finished design.

It is essential that all areas of the design connect to one another with stitching in order for the design to remain intact once the stabilizer is removed. After removing the stabilizer, the remaining thread lace can be applied to a garment or used for home decorating purposes in a number of innovative ways. Used alone, thread lace doilies or coasters are an elegant accent. Strips of thread lace can be used in place of fabric in pieced sections, or used as fringe along the edge of a garment, curtain, or fancy linens.

MATERIALS

- Heat-sensitive stabilizer.
- Fine decorative threads, suitable for both needle and bobbin.
- Decorative machine sewing threads, such as rayon or cotton embroidery thread or metallic thread.
- Heavier threads, suitable for decorative bobbin stitching.
- Soft brush.

∿∿∿how_to Sew Thread Lace

1 Trace or draw design onto heat-sensitive stabilizer. Wind desired heavy thread onto bobbin; set machine for decorative bobbin stitching (page 84). Working from wrong side, outline major design elements, using free-motion decorative bobbin stitching. Change thread colors as necessary.

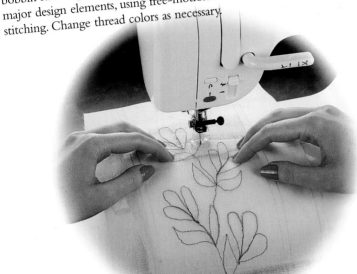

2 Set machine for free-motion straight stitching. Working from right side, fill in design elements with small overlapping loops and circles. Change thread colors as necessary.

3 Fill in background areas around major design elements with small overlapping loops and circles, catching edges of design elements with stitches.

4 Add accent lines of free-motion straight stitches or loops and circles as desired. Add any design elements that will hang free, like fringe, along lower edge.

5 Remove stabilizer, following manufacturer's directions. Brush away residue with soft brush. Press lightly from wrong side.

EMBOSSED VELVET

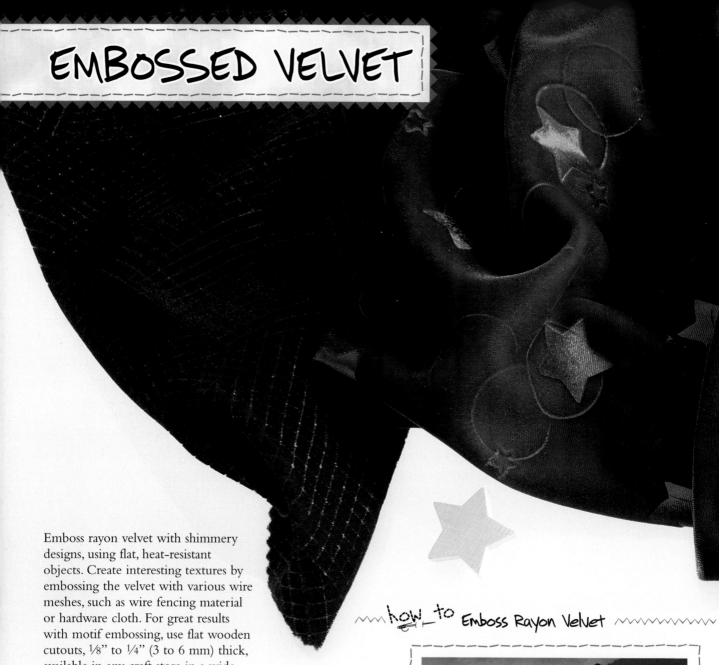

Emboss rayon velvet with shimmery designs, using flat, heat-resistant objects. Create interesting textures by embossing the velvet with various wire meshes, such as wire fencing material or hardware cloth. For great results with motif embossing, use flat wooden cutouts, ⅛" to ¼" (3 to 6 mm) thick, available in any craft store in a wide assortment of shapes and sizes. Use embossed velvet in small doses for an accent on pieced garments. Emboss large areas of the velvet to create unique decorator fabric.

MATERIALS

- Rayon velvet.
- Heat-resistant embossing material, such as wire, flat metal hardware, hardware cloth, rubber stamps, or flat wooden cutouts.
- Iron; press cloth.
- Flat, hard raised surface, such as a block of wood.
- Spray starch.

how to Emboss Rayon Velvet

1 Place embossing material on flat, hard surface. Place velvet facedown over embossing material.

98

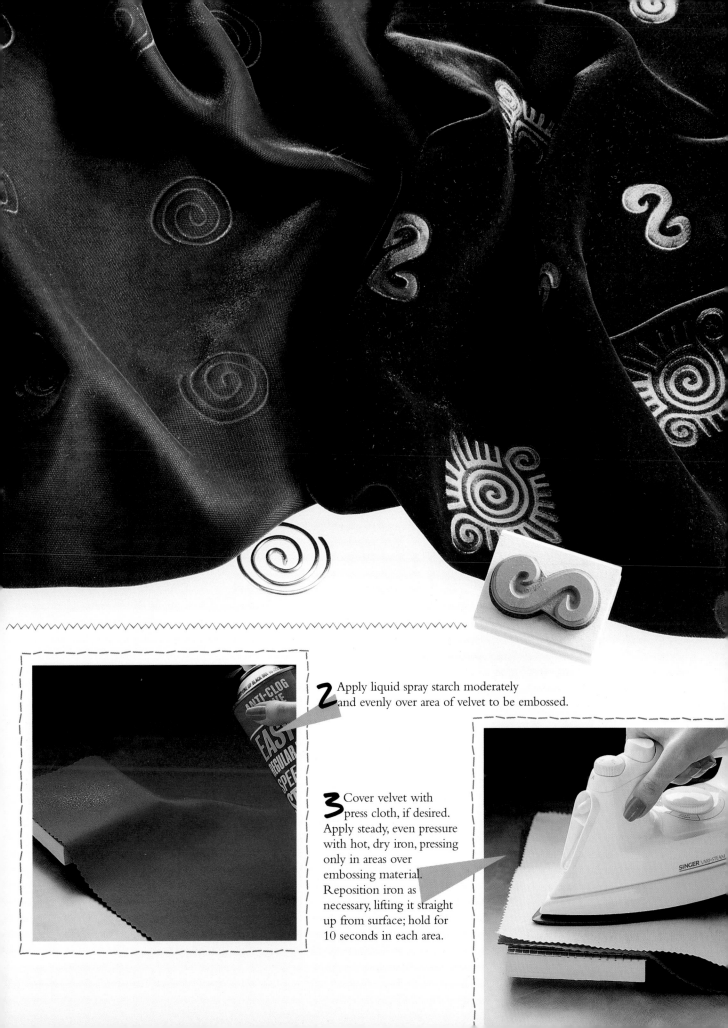

2 Apply liquid spray starch moderately and evenly over area of velvet to be embossed.

3 Cover velvet with press cloth, if desired. Apply steady, even pressure with hot, dry iron, pressing only in areas over embossing material. Reposition iron as necessary, lifting it straight up from surface; hold for 10 seconds in each area.

DEVORÉ

Fiber Etch® fabric remover, manufactured by Silkpaint Corporation, is used in innovative ways to create *devoré,* or cutwork effects, on plant fiber fabrics. The acidic nontoxic clear gel dissolves plant fibers, such as rayon, linen, cotton, and ramie. It does not affect protein fibers like wool or silk, or any synthetic fibers. This allows you to create interesting effects on some blended fabrics that contain 50% plant fiber and 50% synthetic or protein fiber, provided the method of blending involves weaving the fabric with one fiber in the warp and the other fiber in the weft.

Prewash the fabric to remove any sizing or other finish that will prevent the Fiber Etch from working or alter the results. Outline areas to be removed with satin stitching, using polyester or silk thread or metallic thread that has a synthetic base. Stabilize the fabric, using water-soluble stabilizer, paper, or starch. For best results, sew satin stitches at least 1/16" (1.5 mm) wide and tightly spaced with no fabric showing between the stitches. If you prefer, outline areas by using fabric paints or by attaching embellishments with adhesives. Because the gel dissolves the plant fiber, it is very important to read and follow the manufacturer's directions and test this technique on your fabric. Pressing is necessary to activate Fiber Etch, so if it is accidentally applied to the wrong area, sprinkle it with baking soda and wash it out with soap and water while it is still damp.

how_to Use Fiber Etch for Cutwork

1 Mark design on fabric. Place fabric in hoop, if desired. Place stabilizer under fabric. Reinforce design with three close rows of short straight stitches. Satin stitch over straight stitches. Remove stabilizer.

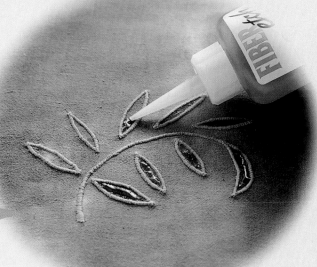

2 Protect work surface with newspapers or paper towels. Apply thin layer of Fiber Etch gel to right side of fabric, in areas to be removed. Dry areas, using hair dryer.

3 Heat iron to setting suitable for fabric. Place fabric facedown on terry towel to avoid flattening satin stitches or other surface embellishment. Press treated areas, using dry iron, until areas become brittle.

4 Rinse under running water, rubbing gently to remove fibers. Allow to dry.

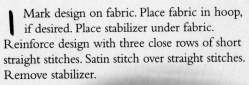

Computer-stitched cutwork (a). Avoid using Fiber Etch® in adjoining areas, since computer-stitched designs usually do not have reinforcing straight stitches around design elements.

Reverse appliqué (b). Place plant fiber fabric over synthetic or protein fiber fabric, right sides up. Satin stitch design, stitching through both layers. Apply Fiber Etch as in steps 1 to 3 on page 101. Fiber Etch removes only top layer, exposing bottom layer.

Reverse appliqué with cutwork (c). Sandwich two sheets of water-soluble stabilizer between two layers of plant fiber fabric, both faceup. Satin stitch desired design, as in step 1 on page 101, omitting further stabilizer. Apply Fiber Etch only to top layer to reveal second layer. Apply Fiber Etch to both top and back to produce cutwork.

No-sew techniques (d). Outline desired areas, using fabric paint, or attach heat-resistant embellishments around desired areas, using fabric adhesive. Follow steps 2 to 4 on page 101.

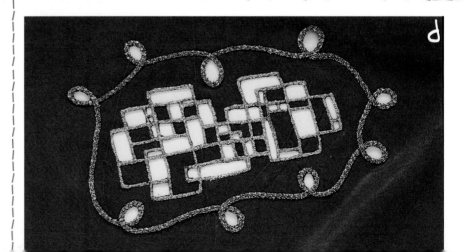

Quilted cutwork (e). Use 100% cotton batting between plant fiber fabrics. Satin stitch around desired areas. Follow steps 1 to 3 on page 101, applying Fiber Etch and pressing on both front and back sides. Fiber Etch removes both layers of fabric and the batting between them.

Frayed-edge cutwork (f). Apply Fiber Etch to small areas, without the confines of satin stitching, paint, or adhesives, for a casual, fraying edge.

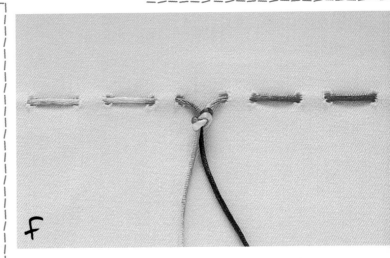

Fabric blends (g). Fiber Etch removes only the plant fibers, creating an "etched" look.

Etched velvet (h). This technique requires velvet with rayon pile and a silk backing. See source list on page 112. Apply Fiber Etch to the wrong side of the velvet, using a stencil or drawing with tip of applicator. Allow to dry, or dry with hair dryer. Place velvet over second piece of velvet, right sides together. Heat-activate with dry iron, using minimal pressure. Rinse fabric to remove pile.

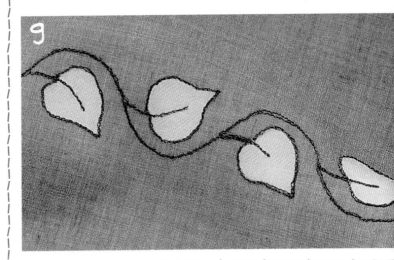

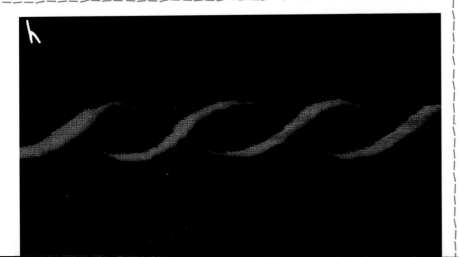

Decorative stitching techniques often require you to mark design guidelines on the surface of your fabric. Browse the latest sewing notions catalogs or walk through the notions department of any fabric store and you will realize that the number of products for transferring designs and marking fabric are staggering. Depending on the fabric and sewing technique you are using, you may find some products to be more useful and appropriate than others. The product should be easy to use, highly visible, and easily removable in a manner consistant with your fabric's care needs. For instance, a water-soluble marking pen is only suitable for marking on washable fabrics and trims.

Transferring methods vary, also, depending on the density and surface texture of the fabric. A light box is a handy tool for lightweight and light-colored fabrics that are easily penetrated by light. Heavy fabrics and dark-colored fabrics can be marked using other methods, such as transfer paper or netting. Highly textured fabrics may require some innovative marking methods, such as freezer paper or thread sketching. When transferring a design, keep in mind that if you will be stitching from the wrong side of the fabric, the mirror image of the design will appear on the right side.

It is a good idea to purchase a variety of marking tools to give yourself options. Always test the marking method and removal on a scrap of your fabric before using it on your project.

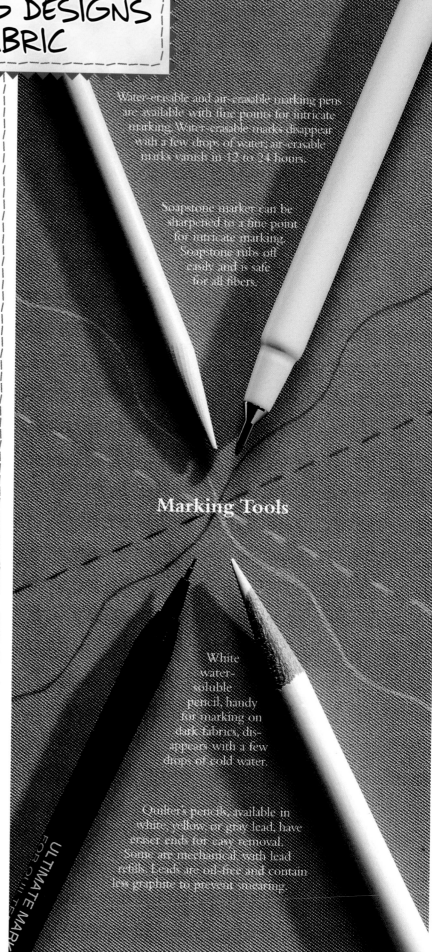

Water-erasable and air-erasable marking pens are available with fine points for intricate marking. Water-erasable marks disappear with a few drops of water; air-erasable marks vanish in 12 to 24 hours.

Soapstone marker can be sharpened to a fine point for intricate marking. Soapstone rubs off easily and is safe for all fibers.

Marking Tools

White water-soluble pencil, handy for marking on dark fabrics, disappears with a few drops of cold water.

Quilter's pencils, available in white, yellow, or gray lead, have eraser ends for easy removal. Some are mechanical with lead refills. Leads are oil-free and contain less graphite to prevent smearing.

ULTIMATE MARK FOR QUILTE

Transfer paper. Select wax-free, carbonless transfer paper in color that will be visible on your fabric. Place fabric on smooth surface with appropriate side up. Place transfer paper facedown over fabric; place design over transfer paper. Secure with weights or pins. Trace simple designs with tracing wheel. Trace intricate designs with stylus or empty ballpoint pen. Trace design lines in systematic order, to ensure that all lines are traced before lifting design and transfer paper.

Water-soluble stabilizer. Trace design onto water-soluble stabilizer. Position stabilizer over right side of fabric; pin. Stitch over design lines, using free-motion stitching techniques (page 88). Remove stabilizer, if desired. Or leave stabilizer in place until decorative stitching is complete; then remove it. This method is especially useful for highly textured fabric.

Netting. Trace design onto nylon netting, using permanent marker. Position netting over fabric; pin. Transfer design by marking over netting with appropriate marking tool.

(continued)

Light box. Trace design onto tracing paper, if necessary, using bold, dark lines. Tape design on light box surface. Position fabric over design as desired; tape. Transfer design, using appropriate marking tool.

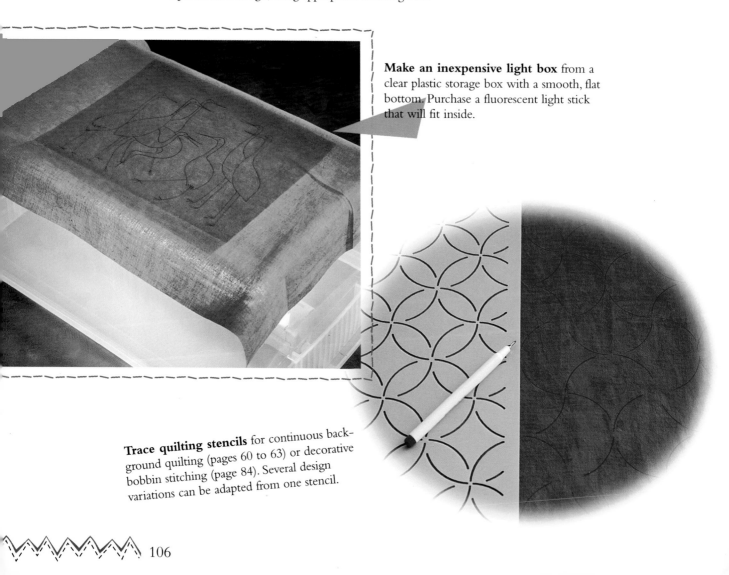

Make an inexpensive light box from a clear plastic storage box with a smooth, flat bottom. Purchase a fluorescent light stick that will fit inside.

Trace quilting stencils for continuous background quilting (pages 60 to 63) or decorative bobbin stitching (page 84). Several design variations can be adapted from one stencil.

Tear-away stabilizer. Transfer *mirror image* of design to tear-away stabilizer or dull side of freezer paper. Position stabilizer on wrong side of fabric; pin. Or press freezer paper, shiny side down, to wrong side of fabric. Stitch over design with decorative bobbin stitching.

how_to Draw a Mirror-Image Corner

2 Place a rectangular mirror on the angle line, perpendicular to the graph paper. On another piece of graph paper, draw the corner as you see it in the mirror.

1 Draw the design on graph paper. Determine the location at which you want the design to turn the corner and the angle of the corner. Draw a line through the design at the determined angle.

STABILIZERS

Many of the decorative stitching techniques utilized by fabric artists require that the fabric be stabilized in some way during the stitching process. Stabilizing provides optimum stitch quality without distortion and prevents the fabric from puckering. An assortment of products are available, each designed for various fabrics and sewing techniques. Read and follow the manufacturer's directions and make a test sample, to be sure that the product is right for your fabric and technique.

RinsAway™
WATER-SOLUBLE BACKING

Tear-Easy
The Professional's Choice
Soft. Light. Tear. S...

Palmer Pletsch
PerfectSew
WASH-AWAY
FABRIC STABILIZER

SULLIVANS

FABRIC STABILIZER

MACHINE EMBROIDERY
...AKING • BATTENBERG •
...OM SEWING • APPLIQUE •
...ES OUT COMPLETELY

...ABLE. HARMFUL IF INHALED
...UNDER PRESSURE
...cautions on back panel
...(400G) NET

$ 3.50
Item No. 840-01

Heat-Away™
Brush Off Stabilizer

Heat with iron | Brush off

Sulky®

Special heat-sensitive woven fabric that disintegrates with a hot iron, then brushes away easily. It's like muslin that vanishes.

Great for:
• Decorative Stitching
• Monogramming
• Battenberg Lace
• Cut Work & Fabric
• Lace ...
• Embroidery
• Machine Applique
• 3-D Applique
• Special Effects
• Delicate Fabrics
• Corduroy & Velvet

Water-soluble stabilizers, available as transparent films or lightweight fabrics, are designed to be used on either side of the fabric. They can be placed under the fabric like tear-away stabilizers. Or designs can be drawn on water-soluble stabilizer and sewn from the right side of the fabric. Some brands disappear with a light spray of water; others require soaking, making them suitable for washable fabrics only. Embroidery hoops and rings are often used, alone or with other stabilizers, to keep the fabric taut while stitching.

Liquid stabilizers stiffen the fabric itself, much like starch. They are either sprayed onto the fabric or spread on with a soft paintbrush and allowed to dry. Drying time can be shortened by using a hair dryer or pressing with a press cloth and hot iron. After stitching, the stabilizer is washed out of the fabric.

Tear-away stabilizers are placed under the fabric for techniques like machine embroidery and appliqué, when the stitching is done on the right side of the fabric. After stitching, the stabilizer is easily torn away. Any stabilizer trapped under stitches must be left there and, with some products, may wash out during laundering of the garment. Tear-away stabilizer is available in sheets or on rolls, as a paper product or a synthetic. Some brands are thinner than others, designed for very lightweight fabrics. Two or more layers of stabilizer may be necessary to achieve the desired stability. Another brand, designed for knits and slippery wovens, is temporarily heat-fused to the fabric before stitching. Household products like coffee filters, typing paper, freezer paper, or adding machine tape can also be used as tear-away stabilizers.

Heat-sensitive stabilizers brush or flake away when they are pressed with a hot, dry iron. Suitable for thread lace (page 96) or other nondimensional work, heat-sensitive stabilizers can be used on the right or wrong side of mediumweight fabric.

Index

Sources:

Clotilde, Inc.
(800) 772-2891
Fiber Etch®; marking tools;
notions; catalog available

Colorful Quilts and Textiles
2817 North Hamlin
Roseville, MN 55113
(612) 628-9664
contemporary prints; hand-dyed
fabrics; 78/76 muslin

Creative Fibers
5416 Penn Avenue South
Minneapolis, MN 55419
(612) 927-8307
felting supplies

Depth of Field
405 Cedar Avenue
Minneapolis, MN 55454
(612) 339-6061
natural yarns; felting supplies

Detta's Spindle
2592 Geggen-Tina Road
Maple Plain, MN 55359
(612) 479-1612
felting supplies

G Street Fabrics
(800) 333-9191
quilting stencils; fabrics

SCS
(800) 547-8025
Madeira threads; catalog
available

Silkpaint Corporation
P.O. Box 18
Waldon, MO 64092
(816) 891-7774
Fiber Etch; fabrics for devoré

Thai Silk
(800) 722-7455
silk fabrics, including velvets;
samples available

Web of Thread
(800) 955-8185
decorative threads; catalog
available

COWLES
Creative Publishing

President: Iain Macfarlane
Group Director, Book Development:
Zoe Graul
Creative Director: Lisa Rosenthal
Senior Managing Editor: Elaine Perry

Project Manager: Amy Friebe
Senior Editor: Linda Neubauer
Senior Art Director: Stephanie Michaud
Art Director: Mark Jacobson
Copy Editor: Janice Cauley
Researchers: Arlene Dohrman,
Phyllis Galbraith, Bridget Haugh,
Linda Neubauer, Coralie Sathre,
Michelle Skudlarek, Nancy Sundeen
Lead Project & Prop Stylist: Coralie Sathre
Project & Prop Stylists: Christine Jahns,
Joanne Wawra
Lead Samplemaker: Phyllis Galbraith
Sewing Staff: Arlene Dohrman,
Sharon Eklund, Phyllis Galbraith,
Bridget Haugh, Teresa Henn,
Valerie Hill, Virginia Mateen,
Carol Pilot, Michelle Skudlarek,
Nancy Sundeen
Senior Technical Photo Stylist: Bridget Haugh
Technical Photo Stylist: Andrea Jensen
Studio Services Manager: Marcia Chambers
Photo Services Coordinator: Carol Osterhus
Senior Photographer: Chuck Nields
Photographers: Dennis Becker, Rex Irmen,
William Lindner, Rebecca Schmitt,
Joel Schnell
Photography Assistants: Andrea Rugg,
Herb Schnabel, Greg Wallace
Publishing Production Manager: Kim Gerber
Desktop Publishing Specialist:
Laurie Kristensen

Production Staff: Eileen Bovard, Curt Ellering,
Laura Hokkanen, Kay Wethern
Consultants: Margaret Andolshek,
Anna Carlson, Marian Hehre,
Candy Kuehn, Lin Lacy, Barb Prihoda,
Katherine Tilton, Joan Wigginton,
Julann Windsperger
Contributors:
American Efrid, Inc.; Clotilde, Inc.; Coats
& Clark Inc.; Conso Products Company;
DMC Corporation; Dritz Corporation;
Dyno Merchandise Corporation; Exotic
Silks; Fairfield Processing Corporation;
Hobbs Bonded Fiber; HTC-Handler
Textile Corporation; June Tailor, Inc.;
Madeira; Offray Ribbon; Olfa® Products
International; Speed Stitch, Inc.; StenSource
International, Inc.; Sulky of America;
Wm. E. Wright Company

Printed on American paper by:
R. R. Donnelley & Sons Co.
01 00 99 98 / 5 4 3 2 1

Cowles Creative Publishing, Inc. offers
a variety of how-to books. For
information write:
Cowles Creative Publishing
Subscriber Books
5900 Green Oak Drive
Minnetonka, MN 55343